Just Words

...for whoever needs it.

www.justmikethepoet.com

Just Words

Not poetry, not floetry, the following are just words.

Just nouns. Just adjectives. Just prepositions. Just verbs.

What you do with these words is your choice. You're not being asked to love it or leave it.

The goal is to inspire progress; it's up to you to put forth the effort to achieve it.

The agenda is to change a life or two, please note you might not relate to this work in its entirety.

The only desire is that you gravitate to a certain passage, that it may offer comfort or inspire thee.

These are just words, not created to establish popularity on social networks.

Just words to network with individuals whose hearts are so heavy it makes their chest hurt.

This is not a gimmick to establish net worth; each passage is written with a purpose.

A wake up call. A sleeping pill. Motivation for those who believe without wealth, life is somehow worthless.

Spiritually motivated, but not biblical, can be read in synagogues as well as churches.

Not prophecy or philosophy, just a few words to make the evils that dwell among us nervous.

The evil I speak of may very well lie beside you, in your community or in your home.

Don't doubt that it may live inside you; realize it may take just words to get them gone.

You must leave what troubles you behind you. The prerequisite for a prosperous future is a plagued past.

These are just words from a man with flaws. These are not stones; I assure you, my house is glass.

A picture may be worth a thousand words, but my goal is to use a thousand words to paint a picture.

It's up to you to make the light bulb come on; my words are just the switch and fixture.

May these words provide you with courage to change course and proceed in different directions.

Whether it is as simple as sex with protection, or giving rejection versus love and affection.

I want these words to speak to you personally, instead of being applauded publicly and recognized.

If you read "Just Words" in its entirety and nothing has spoken to you, then I apologize.

Editor's Remarks

I assure you, this book is more than a simple compilation of "just words"; the title is merely a modest reflection of its ever so humble author. On his behalf, I declare, there is an abundance of inspiration for change within these pages—to do better, be better, and to encourage the "better" in others, that it may be stirred up and shared with the world.

Written to raise awareness regarding many troubling, yet routine facets of every day issues within the lives, hearts, minds, and communities of people everywhere, this book is the perfect prescription for its time, and will surely offer a healing for many types of individuals. There is something for everyone inside—the broken-hearted, the glamorous, the used and abused, the hustlers, the underappreciated hard workers, the dreamers and achievers, and so many more.

Sometimes confronting the ugly truth can be difficult, but often times it is the first step in acknowledging the beauty behind every individual's uniquely imperfect design. This book is not to judge nor condemn any one person's way of living, but rather to present an alternative way of thinking about how circumstances are interpreted and decisions are made. His poems possess an appropriately integrated balance of intellect, complexity, humor, wit and rhyme to inform, educate, entertain, and motivate, all at the same time.

It has truly been a pleasure to assist in the creation of such an inspiring work of literature and I can only hope that readers everywhere will be equally inspired. Thank you Mike, for the opportunity to help present your gift to the world!

Meloni C. Williams

Contents

A Letter to Hip Hop

Is Hip Hop the reason kids grow up without a dad?

Are the bottles paraded in clubs more attractive than the ones pulled out of baby bags?

They don't know Jesus, but they know Jeezy. What are we teaching them?

We need to put Maya Angelou on the radio because clearly the music is how we're reaching them.

Our youth have the right ideas, just applied in the wrong direction.

A flash mob is a beautiful thing when the agenda is progression.

Hip Hop is supposed to be the voice of the people, but my words have yet to be spoken.

Your biggest weapon is the one that lies on your shoulders, not the revolver that you're toting.

1 life is too many lost, one year in Philly it was well over 345.

5 year olds know the words to "6 foot 7," but not "I Believe I Can Fly."

Gone are the days of the songs of praise, asking God to bless the child that has his own.

Now it's "God bless the child that doesn't have both parents in the home."

My challenge to the rapper: be mindful of what you spit.

The industry doesn't have a dog in this fight; they are the captains of this slave ship.

We have traded Negro spirituals for punch lines that might be lyrical.

There was a time that Hip Hop fed the soul. Now, some of these new rappers are cooking up cereal.

I just want my music back full of soul, meaning and purpose.

The beats have the potential for musical greatness; unfortunately the lyrics are quite worthless.

We give "Rounds of Applause" to women in strip clubs, who want to be rewarded with ones for having their ass out.

Though we don't clap for single mothers who work all day and still find time to take the trash out.

While parents are out there "Loving the Crew," there is a child home alone tonight.

Furthermore, if they're asked to go out tomorrow, the answer is probably "HELL YEAH FUCKING RIGHT."

So, if "You Only Live Once" and you're for sure that's the motto,

put the Rozay to the side and these words you should swallow.

Baby Fever

I don't want to sound crazy, but I'm not ready for a baby.

I want the birth of my first child to be one of the last gifts of love I provide to my lady.

54% of children are raised by a single parent. Having both Mommy and Daddy is no longer the majority.

So in order to not be part of this statistic, I must establish some priorities.

First, I want us to be alone.

Then, I want us to build a home.

Then, I want to have a tasteful, yet simple wedding with all of our family, and after the reception fly to Rome.

I'm too old to be a "baby's father." I'm too stingy for joint custody.

My first born will be the reflection of me finding the love of my life, not the result of who was good at lusting me.

Some might say this is impossible, but at one point so was walking on the moon.

I refuse to jump into fatherhood without first jumping the broom.

The woman I jump with doesn't have to be the prettiest in the room because I'm smart enough to know I'm not perfect; why do you think they call us the "groom"?

So grooming I will do, with my bride standing beside me.

I won't rush the situation, haste makes waste—I'll let it find me.

I don't have to find it soon, as long as when it does come it stays forever.

May its bond be so unbreakable in any storm, we both can weather.

I don't want to bring a child into a situation that lacks foundation and stability.

Sex without love is just exercise. Her fertility then is futility.

So responsible I will be—always conscious of using contraceptives.

Just because we have the tools doesn't mean we need to use them, so it's a must to be selective.

This is a promise I made to myself. If I don't keep it, then I must be crazy.

Deep down in my heart I know I'm not ready for a baby.

Get Focused

Fuck being perfect.

Be who you are. Tell them love it or leave it.

If somebody shows you their true colors, then it's black and white, take heed and believe it.

Too many men lose true love trying to chase the asses of the masses.

Too many women have invested more money in handbags than in college classes.

Too many mothers run the street and spend less time with their daughters.

You can't blame her for not learning if you never sat her down and taught her.

Too many fathers are letting mommy handle the responsibility of being both parents.

Too many mothers are letting them off the hook for a couple hundred dollars and a weekly appearance.

Everyone isn't family, too many fake cousins, sisters, and brothers.

The more interesting you make your own life, the less interest you'll have in the lives of others.

Rearrange the focus.

Focus on being a better father. Focus on being a better mother.

Focus on self-perfection instead of public impression and you'll receive focus from others.

If you know more about someone else's problems than your own, then it's time you pack up the surveillance equipment and focus on getting home.

It's okay to follow initially, if leading is what you're ultimately focused on.

Many eyes can focus on one.

Though we were only blessed with two eyes, so be mindful of who yours are focused on.

Your life is never in order enough to comment on someone else's problems.

We need fewer opinions and more solutions. If you're that concerned why don't you help to solve them?

Those with problems are not problematic.

The problem-child is the one who looks for problems in other peoples' attics.

Won't ever air their own dirty laundry because they are in fear of the odor.

Too many people look at life through a wide angled lens.

Bring the focus much closer.

Haters

As long as there is someone in heaven to protect me,
there is no one on Earth whose negativity will affect me.

Misery loves company.
That is one invitation I refuse to RSVP.

Even the devil was an angel once, so be mindful of letting people in—ask to see ID.

The world is full of takers. Some take money. Some take time. Some take a minute to figure out their motive. Be patient and you'll be fine.

The users and abusers will make their purpose known eventually.

You must look past the material attraction, only the real can penetrate you mentally.

The true definition of wealth is not the accumulation of many; it's having just enough of what you need to be able to survive through any. Thing.

One hundred pennies on a scale will weigh more than a dollar would.

The load you carry from having a hundred friends is much heavier than the load a single dollar could. Be.

Don't hate on others, hate on yourself for hating.

Don't hate on the game. Hate on yourself for playing.

Don't hate on the success of others. Hate on yourself for waiting.

We are all given an equal opportunity. So YOU are the only person YOU should be blaming.

Don't hate on hustle. Don't hate on grind. Don't hate on ambition. Hate on yourself for wasting time.

Hate is a disease that lies internally and is a reflection of self-esteem.

Quit being success' nightmare. Wake up and chase yourself a dream.

Truth is, how you feel about me is not my concern, so your personal opinion of me is none of my business.

A hater is the greatest of motivators; if you love your haters can I get a witness?

Whether you're a virgin or diagnosed with the "House In Virginia,"

they're going to talk about you regardless.

Whether your degree is from a community college or Yale, Morehouse or Harvard.

So be comfortable in your own skin and go easy on the make-up.

If they hate on you when they go to sleep, they're going to hate on you when they wake up.

First Impressions

So I was sitting on my porch, minding my own business, when I became an innocent bystander to a crime that I witnessed.

He yelled, "Aye bitch, come here!"

My first thought was, "Damn, another neighborhood domestic."

My attitude became nonchalant; I can't interfere, I must neglect it.

As I watched him run after her while holding his pants up, I said to myself, "If he puts his hands on her in public, I have no choice but to man up."

Her anger invigorated her walk, her pace is now near frantic. He stopped chasing and turned around, which alleviated my panic.

I recognized the perpetrator from around the way, so I approached him.

His response was, "I was just tryna get her number old head." I shook my head and began to coach him.

I said, "Look here young fella, if getting a woman is your aim, under no circumstance are you permitted to call her out of her name!

I know you see it on television and hear it in music, and that's a shame, but respect is learned in the home so it's your father that's to blame."

He said, "I don't got no dad."

Now that's a poem for another time.

I said, “Well if that was your mother walking down the street, wouldn't you want to hear a different line?”

I informed him that women are our greatest assets. They are the creators of life.

So you shouldn't make her a mother if you wouldn't make her a wife, you shouldn't disrespect her and expect her to take it light, and you shouldn't ever chase after a woman unless she’s in fear for her life.

His reply was, "Man, fuck that bitch!" Then, I raised my voice, “There you go with that word!”

Language defines intellect; make better use of your adjectives and verbs.

He replied, "What would you have done? Since you think you’re so smart." I responded, "I would have put a belt on this morning so I could have run faster, for a start.”

Then, I would have asked if I could walk with her, instead of making her change courses.

Real women rarely break their stride; they're busy carrying life’s torches.

Then, I would have introduced myself, gave her a compliment and looked for a smile. Like, “Hello beautiful, my name is Mike. Can we talk for a while?”

If she declines, then that's fine, not every woman you come across will like you, but if you come across a real “bitch” and call her one, then beware, she’s going to bite you.

Now you’ve written yourself a check that you probably can’t cash, and when your mama finds out, there will be 2 women on your ass.

Then, all I'm going to do is laugh because I told you about your speech.

Respect is the difference between getting her number or getting pepper sprayed once within reach.

Respect is due to a dog, but women require admiration, which is the precursor to love, and should come before penetration.

So if you ever come across another woman and her beauty makes you act scary,

take a deep breath, be a man and remove, "Aye bitch, come here" from your vocabulary.

Beauty and the Beast

I was never impressed by superficial.

I never looked for "the look" that could be taken off with the wipe of a tissue.

To those who applaud superficial, may these words pierce you like missiles because even the most beautiful chickens come with gristle.

Why do we put so much pressure on being beautiful?

Applying make-up to make up what isn't perfect; when the reality is you don't have to be beautiful to be worth it.

Our society is one of assimilation and conformity, you look like her and she looks like them and y'all are all boring me.

Those who believe they have mastered this disaster will be ignoring me. Just this once, I ask that an opportunity you afford to me.

Beauty is more than skin deep; it's in the soul, love.

Looks fade and hairs gray when you get old, love. Your outfit's hot, your heels are fire, but your soul is cold, love.

God dealt you your hand for a reason, don't try and fold, love.

You were dealt a King don't try to shuffle the deck to end up with an Ace.

"The look" you should look for has nothing to do with the look of your face.

She protects her beauty by carrying box cutters, razors and mace.

With heels she can't walk in, yet she's running a race.

Running toward beauty and with every step she's losing herself.

Running toward "Loub's" because society has viewed them as an illusion of wealth.

She's got them on, but how she got them is elusive and stealth.

All she knows is she's looking for her prince charming with an "H" on his belt.

She's selling her soul to buy things that are material.

Selling her food stamps to buy Sevens while feeding her children cereal.

How she survives is nothing short of a modern day miracle.

Break ups and nervous breakdowns should make her focus more spiritual.

Foundation isn't applied; it is acquired from the inside. It's true, I wouldn't lie.

Be grounded first. Then fly.

Looking for Love

I'm looking for love. Have you seen her?

I don't mean like. I don't mean lust. I don't mean "wifey." I don't mean a fuck.

I mean love.

I mean one plus one. No extras. Just us against the world, and our love to protect us.

I'm looking.

All I keep finding are these other gigs.

I've met a lot of women I could take home, but none I could take to my mother's crib.

I've had pretty girls: Pretty smart, Pretty bad.

They all wanted pretty "shit": Pretty watches, Pretty bags.

When I didn't provide Pretty with pretty, Pretty got pretty mad.

She switched up pretty fast. So I left her pretty ass.
I'm looking for love—I'm not concerned with a trophy.

Pretty doesn't last anyway.

Ask Kanye. Ask Kobe.

I'm looking for love. Please don't tell me, "Let it find you."

If that's the case, I'm going to sit on my ass and tell love to bring a job, too.

So yep, I'm looking for love.

Back rubs, bath water, and I'm cooking for love. Flights, cruises, and suites—I'm booking for love.

I won't die over stupidity in these streets, but shots could get taken when it's for love.

I know that love exists

because of Martin and Coretta, Will and Jada, Barack and Michelle, Denzel and Pauletta.

So patient I will be, but not because it's a virtue,

but because when you fall in love and don't get caught, that fall right there will hurt you!

Regardless, I'm still looking for love. That will forever be my agenda.

I just hope this time my lover is not a pretender.

I want to make love on Christmas Eve and buy pampers next September.

So I need love to hold me down, not hold me up like suspenders.

I'm looking for love. Have you seen her?

Bad Religion

They were in love, but Religion said they shouldn't be together.

Religion must not know it's hard to pick out a pillow that you're going to sleep with forever.

They prayed to the same person. They just called him by different names.

Both of them were tired of playing games and of their paths being crossed by the lames.

There was a roadblock on their highway to happily ever after.

He could never shake hands with the Sheikh.
She could never meet the pastor.

These worlds have collided for centuries. Though their love caused no blood shed or disaster.

"Sharia" says until he takes his shahadah he would be forever seen as a kafir.

Why does Religion get to determine with whom we get to spend the rest of our life?

She wanted her "rights." He wanted a wife. They both wanted to be at peace with God before they went to sleep at night.

Her only mission was to fear Allah, find her husband and complete her dream.

He didn't necessarily know what that would mean, only that there wasn't an obstacle on Earth he would ever let come in between. Him and Her.

We're taught that at the end of the day, that is all that is supposed to matter.

Until you become a slave to true love, you'll never learn that you cannot do it effectively while simultaneously pleasing your master.

This situation was deeper than the type of bacon put in the pan at breakfast.

Or whether she could go outside with a shirt on that gave notice to her necklace. The one he bought for her.

He was brought up by the Bible; the Koran is what keeps her covered.

How can you choose between being single and a saint, or living in sin by the side of your lover?

It's just scripture. Nothing more than directions on how to create the perfect picture.

Though no picture is perfect. She finally found somebody worth it.

What difference does it make if she prays at the Masjid and he frequents churches?

Either live in ignorance or make a decision. The love they had for each other was deeper than any Religion.

The only reason we have both Christianity and Islam is because variety is the spice of life.

It's bad religion if you have to make a decision between being a child of God and

Husband and Wife.

Daddy's Abortion

Too many baby mothers, not enough wives.

Too many premature ejaculations to satisfy desires for penetration.

Not enough respect for creating lives.

I get the fact that accidents happen, but we're not talking about milk spilling.

We are talking about relationships that end before the 1st birthdays of children.

I'm not judging the past; this is an attempt to educate our future.

If you fall into her womb to create life, be there when they remove the sutures.

I wish some of the boys that didn't want to be fathers knew what a condom was.

It's not an excuse that you didn't know who your father was.

There's not a woman alive that can replicate a father's love.

To the women who deny men their kids, no matter how hard you try, you can never be a father, love.

Society has made it so that being a single mom is somehow okay.

Ask the mothers if they thought they were going to be raising their child alone—the answer is, "No way."

Broken promises birth broken homes. It's all fun and games until her cycle's late.

I meet her after you mistreat her. Now your leftovers are on Michael's plate.

This is daddy's abortion.

Had all the money in the world when it was needed for courting.

20 minutes after her text came, explanations followed about how he couldn't afford it.

Grown man turned Marcus Houston, on his immature shit.

Child support courts play mafia; she puts in paperwork to begin the extortion.

Mommy is daddy now.

Innocent kids don't have daddy 'round.
Mommy's running the home.

Daddy's running the town.

Chicken Coop

Chicken:

Grilled or Fried? Breasts or thighs?

There are thousands of birds that soar in the sky, but it's always the chicken that thinks it's fly.

There are eagles in the air that soar higher than some planes can.

If the only thing you let feed you are chickens, then you'll go crazier than Rain Man.

Chicken is a pseudonym for the average female.

Living below average according to poverty's standards, but somehow simultaneously addicted to retail.

The chicken is where, as a people, we fail.

Anything found anywhere is of no real importance.

How can something be of value when served fried, dyed, and is the feature of every corner store? Chic.

4 wings.

She goes with everyone, from fried rice to Mac and Cheese.

Simple girl, her favorite gifts are Mac lipsticks and 7 Jeans.

Found everywhere, stuffed and cuffed in trucks or bunched in a coupe.

In nightclubs, at house parties, she's made her transition to the street from the stoop.

Some chickens are used merely for breeding.

Whose sole purpose is to provide an egg to the masters they're feeding.

Only to realize that breeding for feeding is different than breeding for love.

Don't be bound by Poppy store clowns, but be free to fly like a dove.

I mean, I love chicken, too, but I'm nervous of Salmonella.

So it's never raw with red bones, curry maybe because it's yellow.

Too cheap to be imitated. Not rare enough to be expensive.

Everyone has tried her. Her list of companions is quite extensive.

Red meat may not be good for you, but even a garbage can gets a steak.

No more being chickens or breeding chickens.

No more chickens on my plate.

How to Keep Her

Every time the two of you go out, treat it like it's the first date.

6 months into it, still get there 10 minutes early, not 45 minutes late.

Still have 2 hour conversations.

Let her come over even during that time of the month.

Don't let desires for penetration make you impatient.

That's how you treat her.

Don't let your attitude change with the season. Don't get an attitude without good reason.

That's how you keep her.

May you prepare a place for her so high on a pedestal, that even heaven can't reach her.

Be her lover and her teacher.

That's how you keep her.

Before your aspirations of spending eternity have her shape shifting from petite to maternity, go see a preacher.

Look her in her eyes before God, and tell her you want to keep her.

Leave the spectators in the bleachers.

Take her someplace nice for her birthday, where no one is wearing sneakers.

Compliment her without making reference to her physical features.

She knows she's beautiful. What she doesn't know is if you're like the rest of them.

So she's like, "I'm not going to give my best to him because once I gave my thighs and breasts to him...

He treated me like a drive thru, and the one time I didn't give him what he needed, he cheated.

So, I've got to throw him my middle finger and the one that's next to it."

Deuces.

Only a coward would beat her.

That's not how you keep her.

Any real man knows that a woman scorned is the most violent of creatures.

Only a fool would mistreat her.

That's not how you keep her.

Don't let your immaturity stain her soul with its impurities.

Be a provider not a liar, all a woman really wants is a sense of security.

That's how you keep her.

My Fellow Americans

The job is not done. Truthfully, it's just begun.

We have taken care of Obama, now we must take care of our sons.

Protect and inspire our daughters.

Now that you have seen the power of unity, take that power and put it towards changing the face of your own community.

One man can never change the course of a country; we need a million more Obamas.

We are living amongst terrorists far more dangerous than Osama.

The real battlegrounds are in our neighborhoods, in our schools, and in our homes.

We can no longer have deaf ears to cries for help. We must now pick up the phone.

We must be more self-motivated, and less dependent on a stimulus.

This election was a Revelation that there is still hope for a Genesis.

Change comes from within. We must first change ourselves.

We can no longer spend our last dollars to validate that we have wealth.

We must put as much effort into education as we do into penetration.

If all we are worried about is who we're screwing,

then we really are screwing ourselves with no lubrication.

My president may be Black, but my streets are still covered in red.

I cannot afford to turn on the news to see another "potential Obama" dead.

Nor can I see the next "Michelle," chasing a deadbeat baby-daddy, instead of her ambitions.

Or watch 9-year-old children in Chinese stores ordering through bullet-proof glass for their nutrition.

Too many mothers are burying their boys. Too many fathers sentenced to life.

Too many baby showers for women whose baby's father has no intention of making them a wife.

Too much excitement in a victory that requires much more from us than a vote.

Obama is by no means our savior—just a small beacon of hope.

You can be Barack, you can be Michelle,

or you can be silent, and four years from now I'll see you in hell.

Big Spender

I thought it went, "Afford everything that you buy."
Now it's, "Buy everything you can afford."

So they can applaud.

If you buy real things for fake reasons, you're just as foolish as the frauds.

No one really cares. Those that do are the ones you shouldn't allow close to you.

What good is looking good, if you don't have money for the things you're supposed to do?

Closet full. Refrigerator empty.

Outside of your mother's house is where you park your Bentley...

because this, too, is your residence.

Fashion is given priority. Family suffers negligence.

I mean, I could spend my last to have things first too, so remind me again what I should be impressed with?

What you need to park is your desire for the materialistic.

Let your desire for achieving the goals you aspire be as fire red as your lipstick.

She looks like a bag of money, but her bag has no money in it.

She waits for him to come get her from her mother's house in his car, which is rented.

So they can go eat somewhere nice like Table 31, Chow's or Chima,

which is cool, unless the check will have him praying for some FEMA.

So you don't have insurance on you beamer?

Didn't realize that driving a 760 would run you $1195? All you wanted to do was ride.

If the response is, "I'm just trying to live," what good is it, if you're living a lie?

Expensive belts. Cheap mattress. You've spent more in Bloomingdale's than you've spent on your Bachelors.

Clothes are more important than college is what you're telling me?

Cable bill is overdue, but you just got gel and acrylic from the nailery.

You stand in line for foams; you stand in line for Jordan's,

but you won't stand up and be a man to the kids you fathered and support them.

The rich will get richer as long as the poor continue to invest.

Make sure you do what's right with your money first, then spend whatever's left.

Think Like a Man

If you're busy thinking like a man, then who is thinking like the woman?

Who is thinking about being the backbone and the nurturer of the children?

If you think like a man, then who is the one that will remind me to think twice before killing?

I want to be with a woman who thinks like a woman, Lord willing.

One whose light shines bright enough to make even the darkest corners seem appealing.

The fire to my ice, whose affection keeps me from chilling.

Women only think like men when they are in the presence of boys,

but there comes a time in every woman's life when she must put away those toys.

...and think like a woman.

Drink like a woman.

She doesn't have to be an AKA,

but it would nice to incorporate my green, with the pink of my woman.

For every night to feel like homecoming.

Instead of you thinking like a man and jumping to conclusions when you hear my phone humming.

Leave the thinking like a man to me.

It sounds like a plan to me; if you're in agreement then take hands with me.

Take a stand with me.

As we bring women thinking like women back into existence.

For there is no greater pleasure than to be in the presence of a woman's persistence,

or a woman's ambition.

With the help of this petition, we can restore women's thinking to its rightful position.

There's nothing like women's intuition.

Give Thanks

Today I woke up with nothing. It was all gone.

When you take things for granted, the things you were granted are taken.

Vision to a blind man is a dream.

Though those with the ability to see often live in darkness.

Silence is deafening, those who are capable of speaking, let not their voice be heard,

but often complain when their prayers aren't answered.

I can't feel my face. Hands become numb when we do not touch everyone within our reach.

When we don't touch ourselves in ways that inspire others.

When we use our hands to break down, and not to build up.

Less Walls. More Bridges.

Less daydreams. More Visions.

Nothing tastes the same. Nothing smells the same.

I should have stopped and smelled the roses,

savored the flavors, not swallowed them whole.

It destroyed my soul.

God gives us gifts; we must use them, not abuse them.

Less is not more—the more we are blessed with, the more dedication we must have to apply our gifts.

Or we will lose them.

To whom much is given, much is expected.

Every gift not utilized is a gift rejected.

Today I woke up with nothing. It was all gone.

The mind is a terrible thing to waste. So is time.

What if you woke up today with only the things you thanked God for yesterday?

Would that be enough?

Next

I'm sorry if the situation you were in before me wasn't meant to be.

I'd be lying if I told you I'm sad he never filled the holes that needed filling because then there wouldn't be any room for me.

Instead of filling your voids, he filled the holes of hoes dressed in the skimpiest of clothes.

Sacrificing his bread and butter for a slice of whoever wanted to roll.

He picked the "he" over "we,"

which worked perfect for me. Now I can begin to apply the pressure that bursts more than your pipes.

I won't feed you the bare minimum. You can have seconds, thirds and even fourths if you'd like.

I want to be more in your life. More than just his encore.

I want to tour and explore what makes you want more out of life.

Morning and Night.

Good things come apart so great things can come together.

Don't take this the wrong way, but I'm glad he dried you up, so we can begin to fix the leaks—both in your heart and your sheets, so when your fire is reignited the result is much wetter.

Better.

I'm sorry you weren't appreciated, rarely stimulated, often penetrated.

You have overcome, worked past the pressure to succeed as woman, mother and lover.

To a man who never valued your beauty unless you were naked and under covers.

The fact that he rolled with his fellas so much, you wouldn't be shocked if being in love with them he was, too.

Sweetheart, he *was* you.

I just hope the past tense stays is the past—defeated by the suspense of our paths.

May our love be as routine as taking out the trash.

I want to be your last.

I want to be the reason you're happy you and him are over.

I wouldn't make you fall for me, if I didn't have every intention of catching you.

Let me be your October.

You can be my June. May our love take us high enough that we look down on the moon.

Soon.

Men with Money

He liked her because she was cute: 5'7, 145lbs, 30 inches of hair—grown organically by a Brazilian.

No children.

She could control the entire room within moments of entering the building.

She would be his new toy, Lord willing.

After hours of chilling, he eventually caught feelings, but was always on his "A" game, and every slip up, when he slipped in, was grounds for Plan B pilling.

She liked him because he had money; his finances ignited the romance.

He took her to France before he pulled down her pants; from that moment on she was stuck in a trance.

He was a dope boy with taste. So her goal was to not be replaced—only to be held tightly by the waist.

She chased.

But no matter how many times he went into his account, it couldn't account for all the time that he went unaccounted for.

To her girlfriends, it's: "he's just busy," but in the back of her mind, it's: "he's probably with some other whore."

Her revenge was retail therapy.

She could work in the mines of Sierra Leone with the way she's able to distinguish color, cut, and clarity.

Behind closed doors, between them was much parody.

Diamonds shouldn't always be a girl's best friend.

She said forget cleaning the kitchen then.

She was walking on mall floors, posting pictures of bags and shoes, for the social networkers keeping score.

A real relationship requires chores.

She ate off his plate, but didn't want to do the dishes.

So when she didn't want to make a mess in his sheets, he called "another one of his bitches."

Moral of the story: don't fall in love with superficial.

Unless those thousand dollar designer bags come with complimentary tissues,

for when disappointments hit you like missiles.

The checks will probably clear, but you might have to make your body bounce.

She thought a man with money would change her life.

Yet, all it changed was her body count.

Baby Mama Drama

She had her turn; she couldn't get it right so he left her.

Now she doesn't know what makes her feel worse, the fact that he won't sex her, or that he regrets her.

She had his baby to stay relevant. Probably should have remained celibate.

While she had him in her back pocket, her front ones were filled with ones because she was selling it.

Out with the highest of bidders, while her child was home with her nigga.

She didn't realize she was killing herself and her baby's father would be the trigger.

Now he has moved on and his heart has found another.

She had a chance to be his everything, now she's just his baby's mother.

She went from being *it* to being *other* because all her bases she didn't cover.

When you take things for granted, the things you're granted get taken.

So it was later for this brother.

Now his new lady is your enemy?

You're a bitter baby mama, and making her life a living hell is where you focus all your energy.

Hate mail. Death threats.

Sober mouths couldn't spit out your cries of regret, so you send him a drunk text.

His new woman is not your issue.

Where you should subscribe is a psychological session,

to treat your periodical passive aggression and newfound feelings of rejection.

I hope this teaches you a lesson. Bring some tissues.

Those two have a bond that not even a baby mama could diffuse.

Those two make beautiful music, while you're at home singing the blues.

Stand by what you do.

He's the man to her that he tried to be to you.

You obviously didn't appreciate it, so it's obvious you two are through.

The Virus

She came for the sex, she left with an infection.

All because she didn't think to ask for protection.

She just saw the erection, and removed her clothing.

He looked clean, but deep inside him, a sickness was growing.

They were barely homies, traded comments on each other's Instagram.

Her next doctor's visit will indeed make her go Instaham.

Internet curiosity has birthed a serious situation.

An entire life altered for a few moments of pleasure provided by penetration.

It was done with no hesitation, contemplation, or prior thought.

Baby girl forgot the lessons sex education and her mama taught.

She wishes a condom was brought. Instead all that was purchased were future doctor visits.

She never imagined it could be her, thought that HIV was for them "project bitches."

Ignorance and arrogance have resulted in a positive test.

That's what happens when you know what is right, and still decide to go left.

All her goals and dreams have suddenly been placed on the back burner.

The sex was a weapon, more dangerous than a black burner.

She can't move, her shoes feel as though she has glue inside.

Another colored girl, contemplating suicide.

Games without protection will surely lead to injury.

I hope the next time you think about going in raw, you remember me.

A poem with a purpose, reminding you it's either condoms or caskets.

For HIV knows no boundaries, it affects the affluent as well as the ratchet.

Attention Deficit

Attention, Attention. Everybody wants it.

The ones who don't have it would kill for it. The ones who've got it flaunt it.

No one is satisfied with being regular.

Not regular like being basic, but regular like not letting everyone know every single move you're making.

Every person you're dating. Every trip you're taking.

To make matters worse, when people say they're tired of hearing about it, you're quick to say they're hating.

Attention makes you weak. Attention makes you sweet.

If you're not getting enough from your current situation, then attention makes you cheat.

Attention makes women sit on sinks in boy shorts with poked lips out.

Attention makes so called men live at home with mom and pull forty thousand dollar whips out.

Men flashing money, women flashing skin, all for the flash of a camera, thus attention deficit is a sin.

Attention, Attention. If the attention isn't special, then the attention isn't important.

Attention is sometimes deadly because "trying to kill shit" could leave you morbid.

This infatuation with attention is creepy, a sign of danger.

Self-evaluate your motives, how could you want attention from stranger?

Be satisfied with the attention you get genuinely, fully clothed, and naturally.

Those who give you attention when it's not expected are the ones who really deserve yours, actually.

Attention with your clothes on, attention with no make-up.

Attention when you least expect it.

Attention when you wake up.

Attention without pictures of bathing suits and boarding passes on social networks.

Attention without going to Neiman's more than you need to, diminishing your net worth.

Attention is a killer, don't be its next fatality.

Social networks are another world. Snap yourself back into reality.

The Break Up

Breaking up is hard to do, but so is being with somebody who isn't right for you.

I told you I would fight for you, stay up half the night for you, take a trip, cruise a ship, book hotels and a flight for you.

But I need more substance at home, since I'm living in a world that's so predicated on material.

You are the 5 star restaurant type, and I'm satisfied with Ramen noodles and cereal.

This is what happens when sex comes first, before you start asking questions.

My focus should have been on picking your brain, instead of you giving me "some" to satisfy my erections.

When you place lust before trust in the order of operation, your physical self is of course satisfied, but your heart becomes impatient.

If you lead with the physical, of course the mind follows.

You might even yell out, "I love you" the first time she does it and swallows.

So while the sex is rock solid, the love is superficial. The same person whose smile used to light up your eyes is now the main cause for your use of tissues.

I can't stay here, but I'll miss you.

Being a man is more than a dick, more than some bread, or moving a brick.

It's being the one she can count on every time, when life's feeding her lessons, making her sick.

Being a woman has nothing to do with the size of your ass.

Or seeing how fast you can run through his cash, or giving spontaneous head, or rolling up grass.

It's about being a team and making it last.

So, if I'm on one page and you're on another, how can we learn life together?

The goal is to find someone who thinks just like you, whose presence is making you better.

When this isn't the case, call an end to the race; it's time for your souls to part ways.

Don't allow someone's presence to outlive their purpose, not by years, not by months, not by days.

Some are for reasons. Some are for seasons. Each has its lessons to learn.

You've tried long enough to make this love work,

it's time you start letting it burn.

D.O.A

As I watched her faith in men deflate, I asked God why He sent her to me so late.

After she sold her soul to the highest bidder, and sexual favors were her rebate.

I wish I could save you.

Rewind your mind to a time before the niggas with game tried to play you.

All my heart, I would have gave you, now I can only give you intelligence, about how trying to be relevant will de-fame you.

You don't do broke niggas, but let the rich niggas break you.

Don't care where they are headed; your only request is that they take you.

If you're on a trip with no destination, baby you're lost.
Listening to that Ricky Ross has got you checkin' for a boss.

If you come across a boss and are not one, then you'll probably just be a worker.

She was looking for a spades partner; he was playing his cards right trying to poke-her.

Mixed signals and mixed drinks led to mistakes.

Be careful who you let in, it doesn't have to be a stranger for it to be rape.

She flaunts her reproductive organ like it was the Pastor's gift to the church choir.

If someone told you sex is what attracts men, then you've been listening to a liar.

Your pussy will never impress me. Show me a diploma.

Or that you're a homeowner.

If all you come to the table with is what you can do to me physically, you don't belong with me you belong on the corner.

What you're selling, I'm not buying.

If I told you different, I'd be lying.

You might get a check for getting wet, but later on you'll end up crying.

Tears from years wasted. Our lives are in different spots.

A friend I can be, but a lover I cannot.

While a boy would grab a condom, I prefer to clutch my Bible.

I couldn't save her though; she didn't want to be saved.

She was Dead On Arrival.

Why I'm Single

Why the hell am I single? The answer everyone wants to know.

Simply put, I'm not just opening up my car door for whoever wants to go.

I'm not planting my seed in soil, if there's no potential for it to grow.

Trust me, when I find the one, the entire world will know.

Until then, my goal is to work toward creating, maintaining and sustaining a better me.

I want to be with someone who's by my side, no matter what the weather might be.

I've made the transition to begin wishing for longevity.

I have no problem waiting until I'm 30, if we're together till I'm 70.

I'm single because I won't be a prisoner to insecurity. She must understand that my popularity will never affect my maturity.

I'm single because I refuse to settle for less than what I expect. My heart is my biggest asset, so it's what I must protect.

I won't sacrifice it for physical gain, and pointless offers for sex.

I won't profit physically off of love and leave my soul in neglect.

I'm single by choice.

Although my character has made a few inquire.

I don't want to be in a relationship; I want to be inspired.

I don't want to be interrogated because those who came before me were liars.

I want you to understand that he was a bottom feeder, and my level of love is significantly higher.

I'm single because I've tried "taken," and who I took, took me for granted.

So I took my talents elsewhere because all she took was advantage.

I'm single because of my standards; I won't bend or lower the bar.

The way my lineup is looking today, I'll probably be single tomorrow.

I'm single in my living room, not single fishing in bars.

I'm single until I find someone worth giving the world to, while making love under the moon,

I'll treat her like a star.

I'm single because I know what love feels like.

I won't do it again unless it feels right.

That doesn't mean because it feels tight, because wrong for me, she still might. Be.

Good Bye

Sometimes goodbye is the best part of the relationship.

A relationship might not be what you were in.

It could have been just relation-shit.

Sometimes growing up means growing apart and that's expected.

A real man would understand, an insecure one will reject it.

You're only given one heart and it's up to you to protect it.

Why be married and mundane, when you can be single and eclectic?

Don't let love make you dumb.

You've got a race to run. They don't have to run it with you—they just have to respect it.

Our fear of being single traps us in relationship prison, imaginary confinement.

Your heart is your most valuable asset, not to be bartered or consigned with.

I'm not a magician. I can't bring your heart back to life, or bring back the night that stuff went left with your Mr. Right.

Y'all fight. I don't.

He broke promise after promise.

When he was questioned, he left you with a negative impression: disrespectful, liar, dishonest.

I won't.

My presence is only to make you better. I'm that warm sweater in winter weather and fall wedges that are light as feathers.

You look at us like, "it's whatever."

I want to treat you like my you're my last.

But you treat me like I'm your past.

Immaturity has led to the security of your heart, pocket book, and ass.

Don't mess up a good thing by confusing it with another.

I want to be your provider, homie, and lover.

Your company when under the covers.

I promise to follow orders like, girlfriend, fiancé, then mother.

We can't even get started because from your old ways of thinking you haven't departed.

I'm the prisoner of crimes that he committed; guilty by association, in need of a pardon.

But more than that, I need a partner. One in crime, you can keep the punishment.

You thought love wasn't supposed to hurt, but I'm here to tell you that what you were in wasn't it.

Martin's Dream

Is this Martin's Dream? More like a modern day nightmare.

Malcolm's "By any means" has grown folks who walk home alone at night scared.

What happened to those who fight fair?

We've traded handshakes for handguns, and we won't take care of our damn sons.

Daughters aren't doing that much better; babies are having babies to escape mommy's Section 8, to move into their own slice of government cheddar.

Young girls are scraping up their knees for street pharmacists with no degrees.

She's proud that he's in the "trap," but she doesn't realize she's the cheese.

Somebody save us, please! The answer isn't Obama. Self-respect is taught at home. We need more ass whoopings from our mamas.

Mama is in these streets, while her daughter is in the sheets, trying to recreate the love her father never gave to her, with these boys that call her a freak.

Soon she'll be called mother, for she's a kid having a kid, and will most likely be a single parent because her child's dad is doing a bid.

The streets have taught him that selling drugs is how you achieve "doing it big."

This lifestyle is bigger than your neighborhood; it's systemic across the grid.

Did we forget that we crossed the bridge?

We are the survivors of the middle passage. Ancestors died to "give us us free." How'd we let lack of motivation become our master?

Outside my window is natural disaster! 9/11 meets Katrina, meets Super Storm Sandy; I pray that this poem is like FEMA.

A place to which the soul may escape. May it make you momentarily a Martian. Let this poem be a peaceful night's sleep to school-aged dreamers, so they too can dream like Martin.

Wake up with strength like Malcolm, with patience like Brother Job. Instead of praying for record deals and jump shots wetter than Kobe.

I pray I see this before I'm old. Reality has set in. Success for Black men has become black cards, fast cars, automatic weapons, and pretty girls that get in.

Martin is turning in his grave.

One Republican president away from being cotton picking slaves.

Too many fathers in a cage. Too many mothers home enraged.

That's not even half the battle. We have a new terrorist and it's called AIDS.

Foolish

She applauds herself for being real a "down ass bitch."

Counting ones, hiding guns, real "down ass shit."

Familiar with the lingo: racks, traps, gats, bricks.

Does she do it for the love, or for the bags, stacks, and Sak's trips?

You love when he buys you red bottoms, but how will you feel once the Feds got him?

Is he with you because of you? Or does what you do while you're in bed got him?

What good is being a rider, if the destination is stupidity?

"High off life" is what she calls it. Well, here's your moment of lucidity.

You say that you're just living; well what good is it if you're living a lie?

You say you're "holding him down," but if he really loved you then he would let you fly.

Sometimes the responsibility of a rider is to suggest we pull the car over and park it.

There's a conversation to be had, I think it's time you two should spark it.

Urban soldiers are getting clapped like erasers, I think it's time you two should chalk it.

These rides are material vessels, so how about you both get out and walk it.

In addition to being the rider, is the obligation of being the voice of reason; please provide it.

If your requests go neglected, then the relationship, you should divide it.

These streets have an expiration date—that's not a myth—it's truly logic.

Put the brick down and pick a book up, say, "farewell" to the corner and "hello" to college.

Thirst success, hunger knowledge, for they are prerequisites for power.

One can never be truly hard as long as they continue playing with powder.

If he rejects his rider's request, and calls your ideas inferior,

reconnect with your own reflection, if you need help then here's a mirror.

What do you see?

His new rider might say you were inferior,

I would take that any day over co-defendant or co-conspirator.

Love Bank

You can't request a withdrawal, if you don't make a deposit.

People want credit for services, but don't understand this logic.

Your statements are personal and your account should be treated as private.

When they see that you're eating, they'll be fraudulent in an effort to rob it.

I'm not talking TD Bank or Police and Fire; I'm a representative of the Bank of Love.

We're not for everybody, but if you're the right one, we'll fit you like a glove.

Let me give you a flyer, free checking: that means, "I'ma let you check for me, but you're going to need more than some ASS-sets before you will ever get a check from me."

Free lines of credit, no questions asked. We bank with trust. Responsibility is all we ask. So don't abuse the privilege and mistake us for lust.

Yes, lust might be cooler, but the value is superficial. Some have put their all into them, and the only thing you get in return is declined and some tissues.

The Bank of Love.

Established in '84, which makes us mature. No discrimination. It doesn't matter if you're rich or poor.

No minimum deposit. No hidden fees. No ceilings or floors. We just ask that you don't show your ass or we'll show you the door!

I'm curious. What's your current banking situation?

Does it require patience and accommodation before they handle your situation?

Long lines lead to frustration when you're in need of penetration. Come where you're handled with care, all transactions free from aggravation.

If you're not appreciated, it makes banking with trust hard.

So be wise with where you deposit your funds. Don't end up with a Rush card.

Banking is everything, invest in Love; I promise we're worth it.

We're stable. We won't need a bail out in case you are nervous.

That's my time. The choice is yours. Thank you for listening.

Invest in Love. Let us show you what these others are missing.

Dear Mama

For all the mothers that do it alone, I respect you. Never let your baby's father or his failures as a parent affect you.

You're special.

I know you don't hear it enough, and some nights while the kids are asleep, you're daily struggle makes you start tearing up.

It pays off when they say, "I love you, mommy." I know that cheers you up.

Mommy is daddy, too. It's not ideal, but it's ok, you just went fishing and caught a crab. Remember next time to bring the old bay.

All jokes aside, the joke's on him for missing out on a blessing.

Contemplate how many females don't get the opportunity to create life, when your creation has you stressing.

Nobody ever said it would easy, but sometimes children make it all worth it.

Their love is what helps you make it through because Lord knows, life is far from perfect.

There isn't a training or certification that comes with puberty.

Sex education doesn't teach boys to be fathers, just how to not spread disease throughout the community.

You made a baby with a baby that called you baby, though the result was grown.

The one who promised they'd always be by your side has up and left home.

I know this isn't the picture you painted, but it's okay mommy, life goes on.

You're satisfaction comes from knowing that your kids are happy and the lights are on.

God has blessed you now with a love that's unconditional. One that provides you with simple pleasures, not reasons to carry mascara, foundation, and extra tissue.

Life gives its toughest issues and hardest battles to its strongest soldiers.

It's all going to work out; they say it gets easier as the kids get older.

Maybe not easier, but they definitely become a helping hand.

There is not a woman on Earth that isn't capable of raising a child without the help of a man.

Don't let society trick you into believing that your home is broken.

It was just put together differently.

How men can walk the Earth knowing they have children who need them is the saddest of mysteries.

Working Woman

I want you.

Naked. Covered only by covers.

You've been a working woman all day. Tonight, be my lover.

Once, twice, three times if you can take it. The sex that women dream about, I promise we will make it.

Run your bath water. Wash away the day's dirt.

I want to go deeper, wider, provide you beautiful pain—one that can only be compared to giving birth.

Lay with me. Stay with me. Until bones get old and your hairs gray with me.

Let's make love-making a sport. Come play with me.

I know you've got to work tomorrow, and you just got your hair done, so I'll be cautious.

I just want to put in as much work in pleasing you, as you put in at the office.

I'm not afraid of overtime.

Or that little bit of baby fat; if it wasn't cool Kimora wouldn't have turned it into a clothing line.

I want to control your spine, the way your nine to five controls your time.

At work, he controls your mind, but once you're home, you're mine.

My working woman, you're perfect woman.

Giving up half my check, so you can keep all of yours has never been so easy because you're worth it woman.

You're worth it woman, you inspire me to soar to new heights of successful.

Remind yourself that you have a good man to come home to when working seems oh so stressful.

As long as you continue to be my working woman, I promise to work for you.

I promise to provide, protect, and respect you, and to be the epitome of loyal.

My working woman,

May your days be long enough that you can't help but miss me,

but short enough that I still feel the imprint on my cheek from this morning when you kissed me.

As long as you don't diss me, we can do this until we're fifty.

Are you with me?

Baby Father Drama

Why am I the bad guy?

You were the "old enough to hit her raw,"

but "not old enough to be a dad" guy.

I was the "shoulder to cry on," “ride to the market,” and “Can I come over because I'm sad?" guy.

Now that you find out I exist, you're the,

"go through her phone, texting, threatening, probably do some sucker shit like try and hit her because you’re mad" guy.

It's really you that has the problem.

She only calls me when you act stupid.

If you stop acting stupid then she stops calling.

The telephone threats are just your cries of regrets to make up for the neglect and lack of respect your "baby’s mother" has for you.

Your son sees me more than he sees you.

I have no desire to replace you,

rather prove to him and his mother that neither one of them need you.

You planted a seed in her Earth, but allow other women to feed you.

I hope you don't breed you.

The son of a deadbeat desperately needs a role model.

If not, he's going to grow up thinking it's cool to be you.

You give the streets the attention, and your family the neglect?

You refer to your child's mother as everything but a queen and
give random women respect?

I'm going to refer to you as the dumb guy.

You're missing out on moments to watch your son grow because
you want to be the,

"I just want to have fun" guy.

Out there trapping and you're packing.

You're a "hold your gun more than your son" guy.

Hopefully, 10 years from now you'll try to give your son a high
five,

and he turns around and let's one fly.

What Do Women Want

What do women want? I wish they came with instructions.

Instead of emotional baggage from previous cats that they were once lusting.

When you deal with older women, you battle trust issues and desires for commitment.

When you deal with younger women, you battle immaturity and intellect that's insufficient.

I don't want to have to convince you that my focus isn't penetration.

It's the look in your eyes when you tell me you love me that gives me warm sensations.

I don't want to teach love or preach love. Maybe one day I will reach love.

God's love washes sins away. He doesn't use Clorox, but that's bleach love.

I want 'make love on the beach' love. 'Call off from work to catch up on sleep' love.

I want Barack and Michelle. Not Lisa Turtle and Screech love.

I want strong love. I want bold love. I want that 'keep me warm when it's cold' love.

I want that "damn y'all still together?," through any weather, timeless and old love.

If not, then I want no love.

No kisses, hugs, or affection.

Love is a gateway drug and when taken wrong, can turn to aggression.

Aggression is not as bad as suppression. Can you die from lack of affection?

They say love is in the air. Well, can I get a breeze blown in my direction?

What do women want? I just want one who wants the same.

One that's more satisfied to have a winner, than happy to be in the game.

This question will never get old because every day, a woman's wants change.

I just want a woman who wants me every day.

I'll promise to do the same.

Real?

These days, in a room full of "real niggas" pardon me if I don't fit the description.

Either there was a meeting I missed, or somehow the whole game changed; I no longer mind being labeled as "different."

I don't think the rap song about me has been written yet. What I wear, how I think, where I want to be in 5 years—stuff like that.

People are so caught up in the moment that they have forgotten life is a marathon.

Socially, we've never been more interconnected; everywhere you go there is a camera on.

Don't be so focused on posing for the picture that you remain stuck in the same position.

If you thought I was going to scream, "Fuck bitches, get money" my entire life, then you people truly are trippin'.

The legacy that is our existence is being written with some sections missing.

Somebody has to talk about savings accounts, reality checks that don't bounce, and respecting women.

Trust me, it's cool to cook, read books and go to church, if you need to.

Everybody looks for a place to hide when they're running from the evils.

I want to fly with the eagles, that's why I don't hang around pigeons.

It doesn't have to bring me to my knees before it's seen as a bad religion.

Just slow me up enough that I forget my life has purpose.

There's no majesty in material, so I don't keep track of your accumulations of worthless.

Want to impress me? Mentally undress me.

I'm not perfect, but that's what makes my hunger for success even greater.

The fact that I'm simultaneously being a contributing member to society and not giving a single concern about the feelings of a hater.

Success breeds jealousy, so hate is to be expected.

You need to be grounded; incorporate a mixture of positive and negative to be electric.

Multi-tasking shows maturity. You can still smoke weed and be seen as eclectic.

My mission in life has transformed to being well off and well respected.

Not famous though because Amos was, and look what happened; they ate him.

Cornel, Martin, and Barack, a different CMB, and millions hate them.

Success through motivation and ambition will keep us from being down forever.

Denzel in "Glory" was cool, too. You can't want to be Nino Brown forever.

If I die tomorrow, remember, I was me. Not an imitation or
interpretation of what I hear and see.

My temperament is undefined, but lies somewhere between
Tyler Perry and Spike Lee.

Wise enough to know when to put on collared shirts, but still
appreciates the simplicity of a white tee.

It's impossible to assassinate my character because I'm not an
actor.

I'm just a young Black kid who never wanted to be slave to his
imperfections, only to graduate with his Masters.

The power of that piece of paper is what separates our nation.

If you need motivation, how about your great-great grandmother
who never made it off the plantation; she's waiting.

Her only desire is that her blood has not been spilled in vein.

Leave your grandchildren a legacy not just a couple pictures and
a last name.

The Third Victim

Why is daddy hitting mommy? Do grown-ups get beatings?

Is she lying? Is she stealing? Is she using? Is she cheating?

Does mommy not love daddy? Why is mommy bleeding?

I think I hear her calling for help. Should I go downstairs? Does mommy need me?

Is it my fault? Did I do it? If I did, then daddy I am sorry!

Is it money? I know my birthday is coming up, daddy we don't have to have a party.

I just want mommy to stop crying; she told me crying is for babies.

I don't know why my mommy is crying? Is she cutting onions, maybe?

I don't know what's going on. Why won't mommy stop screaming?

Am I asleep? Am I alive? Am I dreaming? I hope I'm dreaming.

He beats her, mistreats her, but for some reason she stays with him.

Internalizing has her blaming herself for the abuse.
"I just gotta know when to play with him."

Modern day slavery, no 40 acres and a mule though.

Just bruises on top of bruises, but she's still smiling like, "girl, I'm cool though."

Lying to her family, lying to herself, but real eyes realize that past the lies, she's crying out for help.

Daddy hit mommy, Jodi hit Yvette, but they were boys, baby.

What's going to happen when his next reaction happens in front of your baby?

Please leave now because if you hold your peace, you'll probably rest in it.

He brings out the worst in you with his abuse. Why do you continue to put your best in it?

It's not okay to be hit. It's not okay to be treated like shit.

How is it okay for weak males with traits of females to dog you out, to call you "bitch"?

You must think about the third victim, the one in the other room, who's too afraid to open the door.

Don't let the one time he's brave enough to check on his mother be the one time she won't get up off the floor.

Lost

She's lost.

The "Baddest Bitch" searching for a "Boss."

She'll do anything to get him, no matter the cost.
Even if it's selling,

her soul.

To get her wrist cold, and some Louboutins to go with her Levis.

All because they have been telling her she was beautiful since she
was knee high.

Beautiful people deserve beautiful things.

So she began to accumulate a treasure chest full of meaningless
watches, bracelets, and rings.

She'd never speak on the drama they'd bring.

Reality Television has taught us that it's not about who you are,
it's about who you sleep with.

Who you creep with.

They don't care about her story, just how she looks in Victoria's
Secret.

We've failed her. We didn't give her the proper tools, so the
streets just screwed and nailed her.

17 and pregnant, diapers before diplomas.

She signed a birth certificate before signing mortgage papers, she
owns a life, but she's not homeowner.

Another urban solider, fighting to escape poverty.

Daddy can't help with her real estate because he's busy being state property.

She doesn't know the meaning of self-worth.

Loving the crew without loving herself first,

Didn't fully develop feelings yet, but is more than familiar with how being felt up works.

How can you blame her?

No home training, so niggas trained her.

Disrespected and neglected, never knew to correlate the dick with danger.

So it's farewell to Howard, and hello to welfare.

We associate this stigma to that enigma; we need more than some checks.

We need some help here.

Numbers

I talk to 30 women,

23 have kids, 6 of them have 2 or more, 11 of their baby's fathers' are doing "bids."

The oldest is 35, the youngest is 18. One has 30 inches of Brazilian. One has a baldy like Mr. Clean.

20 of them work, the other 10 come up from hustles.

None of them are on trial so trust me, I don't judge them.

I guess they're all getting it from the muscle.

The muscle between their legs is their employer.

One in Med School, 4 do hair, one studying to be a lawyer.

All of them are cute, in some way or another.

One calls me her everything, 3 of them call me their brother.

All of them want time, most of them want mine.

The future is dark for 5 of them, so they're around because they want to shine.

7 have been around for years, 3 of them are brand new.

Some say they are still virgins. Some have been run through.

20 want to be Mrs. Right, 5 want to be Ms. Right Now.

15 want to give me the milk for free, only 2 say I've got to buy the cow.

Some of them know of others, others think they're my only.

I've got to keep like 30 on staff, to ensure on any given night I'm not lonely.

I'm really looking for 1.

If I find her, I swear I'm done.

Somebody to keep me serious, and knows the meaning of fun.

9 of them play a lot. 4 don't play at all.

8 just want my company, 5 want to hit up the mall.

2 of them are divorced. 1 is separated.

I don't really like her, it's just payback because her girlfriend hated.

I think you get the point; I've got options like changing clothes.

My super hero days are over. I'm not into saving hoes.

All of this, to look for love—variety is the spice of life.

I wouldn't make any of the 30 mothers, without first making them my wife.

How does 1 man pick? Who cleans the best? Or rides the best dick?

Who comes with the least baggage, because I pack light on relationship trips.

I would say, out of the 30, 20 have potential.

29 stimulate me physically; with 1 the attraction is purely mental.

I think I've made my decision; all 30 are getting shown the exit.

If I haven't met one that makes me forget about the others, then these feelings are superficial.

So it's only right I reject it.

Get Your Mind Right

When are you going to get your act together?

You're going to need to spend a whole day getting drawn on to cover up those tattoos of your past "whatevers."

You thought love was money. You thought love was trips. You thought love was threatening messages, being disrespected and called a "bitch."

I think you need to call it quits. Your chocolate self needs to subtract the nuts, put a banana in his tail pipe and call it splits.

Don't let money and curiosity get you tricked into meetings.

Every day is Halloween, if you trick when they're treating.

The trick is: people only give away what they don't need.

Don't value what comes in abundance. Baby, your most sacred parts are more valuable than a couple of hundreds,

or a couple of thousands.

and a couple of millions.

No sex for checks, if the asking price doesn't start at a trillion.

All of those could be combined and the offer should still be a waste of time.

The woman God created from my rib should be aware her meat is prime.

So stay away from strays when it's feeding time. Understand that your appetite requires more than niggas feeding you lines.

He should be feeding you time.

Like you, it is precious and irreplaceable; any nigga that thinks it's cool to touch you without permission is surely mace-able.

Your past may be traceable, but your future is well in front of you.

The number of men who have had the pleasure of having you should be merely a fraction of the number that wanted you.

So, what are you going to do? Only God knows what you're going through.

Some parts of life are better walked alone; you don't always need somebody to walk with you.

Bye Philly

Having a gun doesn't make you a killer, no more than a having a basketball makes you Kobe.

My biggest fear is dying by the hands of a man who doesn't know me.

By the hands of a man who thinks he owes me.

All because some female that doesn't even know he exists tends to "joe" me.

This cycle of violence tends to blow me.

I wish it blew me hard enough that I might escape these trials and tribulations.

All I want is a peaceful neighborhood and decent living situation.

Where I could walk my son to the store with no hesitation.

Where my daughter can attend a school where young men provide protection, unaccompanied by desires of penetration.

Where I'm from is the proverbial ground zero.

Where drug dealers, killers, and stealers are praised as heroes.
Where the poets, 9-5ers and college kids are labeled the weirdoes.

If I'm going to make it out, the requirement is deniro.

So I've got to keep pushing through this over-ground railroad.

I thank God every day my bus trips never end at the jailroad.

I pray every day that I don't fall victim to either one of the blocks.

The ones accompanied by cells or the ones that dwell on dirt where caskets drop.

I'm from Philly, where for some people, the best chance they might have to make it out is hitting the Powerball.

Where the adolescent version of ecstasy comes in the same bottle as Tylenol.

To anybody doing anything positive, I'm proud of y'all.

To anybody who hates on success, I'm tired of y'all.

How are we going to defeat the enemy, if we're at war with our own?

Defending streets that destroy our lives, while neglecting our homes.

Where revolvers are problem solvers, so everyone's clutching their chrome.

As much as I love Philly, I've got to leave it alone.

The Reel World

You know what you deserve.

You can't be worthy of the world, but settle for and accept the curb.

Love is the only portion of your life you have complete control over.

You can't award back rubs to people that give you the cold shoulder.

Once you tolerate bullshit, you can't be upset when it's repeated.

What do you think Claire Huxtable would do if she found out Cliff had cheated?

What's happened to us? We went from Florida Evans to Evelyn. Billy D to Stevie J.

Bands never made Michelle Obama dance, but I think she's doing okay.

You're "Living Single" with your "Girlfriends" and currently sleeping with "2 and a Half Men."

Your "Flavor of Love" was a dope boy, until you had his son 3 years ago and now he has 2 and a half in.

Now you're contemplating a "Prison Break." Don't create new love with a has-been.

If you didn't see a future in it the first time, leave it in the past. There aren't anymore "Good Times," and apparently "Family doesn't Matter."

It's all about "Keeping Up With the Karadashians," and getting your ass a little fatter.

"16 and Pregnant" is reality television. "40 Year Old Virgin" is a comedy.

Everybody wants to "Dance with the Stars," but won't take a class in Astronomy.

You're not a "Real Housewife," if you're not married, nor own your home.

You'd rather be a "Bad Girl" and play "The Game." Don't swim in the social media "Shark Tank," create your own.

They've sent us "The Wire," but we've acted like we didn't see it.

So then they began advertising us getting "Locked Up" and still we continue to be it.

No more "Love and Basketball," it's all about "Love and Hip Hop." I wish they'd brought back MLK. No offense to 2pac.

We worry about "Jimmy and Chrissy," "T.I. and Tiny," and the rest of them.

Instead of slicing your own piece of the pie, and movin' on up, like "The Jefferson's."

Let Go

Know when to let go.

Nothing lasts forever.

Not love, not family, and certainly not the weather.

You've got to shovel snow sometimes to appreciate the beach.

The only lesson that can't be learned is the one you don't teach.

You can't complain about things you time after time tolerate. If you wait till the night before the final to study, then you're probably kind of late.

Proper Prior Planning Prevents Piss-Poor Performance.

One day in Planned Parenthood might be better than 18 years of abortion.

You've got to weigh your options. Is it full time or seasonal?

Sometimes you've got to leave before someone gives you a reason to.

If the reason is an act of treason, then you'll be at war with people who were once a friend.

It's only a mistake the first time you allow people to hurt you, simply ignorance if done again.

Keeping your enemies close doesn't always mean you sleep with them.

Everyone needs ground to walk on; they're close when you wipe your feet with them.

It's time to let go.

They call these feelings growing pains. It's better to be lonely than to be with someone whose idea of love will make you go insane.

Take a vacation.

Take back your patience because although it's a virtue, too much patience in the wrong places can do nothing more than hurt you.

You might not be able to help you love, but you can help who you let mistreat you.

Stop looking for substance in certain places because unfortunately some things are simply see through.

Simply speaking, when life gives you lemons, you simply make lemonade.

Though most stay around trying to recreate that "beginning phase."

Run now before you let them get away with murder.

How come you don't to want move, like Rosa Parks, even though you've seen the truth in them, like Sojourner?

No Choice

I need a lawyer. She's trying to kill my daughter.

This is her decision. I'm just supposed to be here to support her.

However, I don't support it. This is the mission God has blessed me with. How could I abort it?

Can you put it in my stomach? Why didn't God give men a uterus? This is ludicrous.

On top of that she wants *me* to pay for it! I swear to God this woman is losing it.

I regret us doing it. Can I write the judge a letter?

"If she just holds her in for nine months Your Honor, then I will hold her down forever."

Why did you even tell me? There are some things you should keep a secret.

This isn't me finding out you cheated. This is the type of grief you go to sleep with.

The sleep from which you wish you never wake up.
Excuse me; I think I have to throw up.

Having sex can be done by children, but the repercussions are for the grown up.

I hate you, and that says a lot because I don't even hate my dad for leaving.

It's never too early to start grieving, especially when she can't even give me a reason.

McKenzie. Not a lick of Irish, but it sounded cute.

I already pictured you this winter, bundled up in your snow suit.

Your first picture with your first tooth.

McKenzie Elizabeth Reid. Yeah, I picked your name out.

I remember the night your mother called me to come create you; I wish I would have never came out.

Well, that I'd gone out, but never came in. I should have made her swallow.

The place where my daughter lives tonight—tomorrow, will be hollow.

At least it will match my soul; my life won't be the same without you.

One day, when I have your little brother I'm going to tell him all about you.

I'm trying to keep it together, but as I'm writing this, I'm really sad.

The consequence of having fake relationships is not having the opportunity to be a real dad.

I always thought of myself as being pro-choice.

Until I was left with no choice.

No opinion to be taken into consideration, no perspective for my connection…

No voice.

Get Back To The Future

We will forever be seen as inferior if we don't reshape public perception from the interior.

To begin the process of progress we must redirect what labels us as problematic to the posterior.

Swallow disrespect and neglect, regurgitate inspiration and autonomy.

Ignorance has made us familiar with full-size and luxury, but uneducated on the economy.

This is to our detriment, prosperity postponed, while we pile on the petulance.

How do we expect things to change in our community with no resonance from its residents?

We need to speak with as much conviction as the justice system administers to the troubled within our communities.

Complacency is a disease. Ambition will grant you immunity.

I look at this Presidential election and marvel at the attention it has erected,

What's confusing me is where these loyal supporters were when Governors and Senators were elected?

It's unfortunate when victory relies on popularity and publicity.

Causal activists are appreciated, but what's required is consistency.

Obama is not our savior—a catalyst for change, possibly.

Instead of inquiring what he will do for you, focus on becoming his prodigy.

The less educated you are, the more vulnerable you become.

Many have no direction as to where they are going because they are clueless of how far we've come.

If we were more educated about our history, our position in the future wouldn't be such a mystery.

Internet Game

I've seen a lot of stuff change because of this Internet game.

It has given the quiet kids a voice.

Put a lot of bench players in the game:

It gave the mediocre girls attention and the unknown boys fame.

I've seen a lot of shit change because of this Internet game.

People log into a site, and forget who they really are.

Change your name, create a bio, now you're a neighborhood super star.

Your "@" name is your block, your favorite rapper or song you sang.

You went from little James Carter to @jroc103swpgangbang.

With every attempt at assimilation, you lose a piece of yourself. It appears that the accumulation of "friends" is the equivalent of wealth.

In competition for titles, but no one is awarded a belt. Women can't see past all the attention because men's motives are stealth.

I've seen a lot of shit change because of this Internet game, people will beg, borrow and steal for some Internet fame.

DM's and inboxes filled with Internet game.

We're slaves to social networks, let's break the Internet chains.

Message to the ladies: don't confuse interest with attention, you're in your underwear in your avi, that's why them fellas in your mentions.

I'm trying to school you. Show some class. Put your assets on suspension.

These silly girls are late out here. That's why they're mind is in detention.

Popularity breeds arrogance. I guess that's the nature of the beast. Shorty got 1000 followers now, she doesn't even speak.

She's your "bestie" on the book, but in life y'all won't even meet.

If you can't stay off the gram for 7 days, don't tell me that you're not weak.

I've never been a fan of the Internet crowd. With their Internet Jordan's, smoking their Internet loud.

Showing their Internet money, faker than Internet smiles, these lions are tame in the streets, log in, and turn Internet wild!

Be who you were before you got here, not your Internet name.

I've seen a lot of shit change because of this Internet game.

Tough Love

It's okay to walk away. If they don't appreciate what you bring to the table, I recommend you don't stay for dessert.

How are you supposed to maintain feelings for someone, when every time you turn around yours are getting hurt?

Time is too precious to waste on people who take your kindness for weakness. Direct them to their seat in the bleachers.

Never "Joe" them; wake up one day and act like you don't know them.

If their presence doesn't add value, subtract yourself and I bet they'll notice.

Some kids learn "the hard way" the hard way.

The Bluff, Marcy Projects, or Compton Boulevard way.

You've got to kick folk out ya life sometimes. Eventually they'll notice the view is quite different from the hallway.

I'm talking Tough Love.

That, "Yeah, I like you and all that, but I don't give a fuck" love.

That, "Hello, yeah I can't talk right now, call you back" then hang up, love.

That, "Don't fuck up love."

Letting a bird out of its cage is one thing, but if they leave it open, you should fly higher than the shit they're smoking.

I'm not joking. Even Jesus flipped a table or two when situations provoked him.

Discipline breeds respect. All is fair in love and basketball.

So when you get that phone call and the number is blocked,
play some D and reject.

Everyone knows absence makes the heart grow fonder.

When you take things for granted the things you were granted
will be removed.

You must always pick self over all else, if ever forced to choose.

Sometimes you win, sometimes you lose.

Never remove your pride for the sake of someone you've come
to love.

Pride wouldn't be in the equation, if they were the one sent from
above.

It's going to get rough; it can still be love even though it's tough.

Text them anyway and tell them to get their stuff.

This way of living sucks, but giving in is not only embarrassing,

it's also 10 times worse than giving up.

Material Girl

Just because you can afford it, doesn't mean it's necessary.

She doesn't make the clothes; the clothes make her.

Selling her soul to get the latest. Saving is not an option.

Why is Old Navy cool for her kid, but it's 'labels only' when she's shopping?

She calls Miami her second home when she doesn't have a first.

Spending tuition on a purse.

She's conscious of it, which makes it worse.

$4,700 bag that will never have $4,700 in it.

Visa, MasterCard and Discover all over their limits.

Spending her cash for street credit. Looking for hood acknowledgement.

I sit back and observe. The first word that comes to mind is: astonishment.

She's a credit whore. Baby girl, only thing you are killing is your credit score.

These streets are filled with takers? What do you need their credit for?

Too much assimilation, not enough originality.

Put the Louie backpack down and snap back into reality.

Red bottoms and a bus pass is a hell of a combo.

I'd rather have some low top chucks and keys to a condo.

$225 for a t-shirt, and walks in heels that make your feet hurt?

Expensive is the celebration of success, you must learn to be cheap first.

Society has robbed us, inspiring this passion for fashion.

Some try so hard to be fly, but really baby, you are crashing.

If everyone tries to be fly, then being fly becomes regular.

Regular shouldn't be expensive, so the cheap are two steps ahead of you.

We try too hard to impress people with the material.

What good is a $300 dinner tonight, if tomorrow you're eating cereal?

Outfit well put together, but home is a wreck.

Looking like a bag of money, but really in debt.

What you need more than a pair of Loubs is to sit and reflect.

Put your debit card down. Write a reality check.

The Ex-Factor

Not All my exes live in Philly, but that's where I'm from.

When I think about why they're my exes, man I swear I feel dumb.

God has truly blessed me with some beautiful women.

I was so busy trying to play the game, I forgot I was winning.

My relationships didn't have God in them, so in actuality, I was sinning.

I know they are reading this now; some are probably grinning.

Maybe not. For the most part, I let them down.

I had queens at home, but my pride wouldn't allow me to provide them with crowns.

They gave me millions of reasons to smile, yet all I would provide was frowns.

Now I'm alone swimming in regret, please pray I don't drown.

It's safe to say my biggest flaw is that I'm a flirt.

When the disrespect is done in public, it causes twice the hurt.

No matter how much stuff you buy, it won't wash away your dirt.

It's a female trait to me, so I believe it's time I pull down my skirt.

I don't want anyone to think because I write poetry that means my life's perfect.

I write to inspire others and in part, to give my feelings purpose.

My mistakes have me feeling like without love, some parts of life are worthless.

I'm 28 with no kids, and no I'm not proud, I'm actually nervous.

If you're my ex and you're reading this, then I apologize.

Love is built on trust and my actions caused major compromise.

If you were sitting here, you'd see the tears roll down my eyes—real tears, no more letting the song cry.

I am human and it's true, we all make mistakes.

When you keep making the same one, then your excuse is fake.

To take me back is a chance you'll probably never take.

The only time I was supposed to make you cry was on our wedding day.

A date we'll never make.

I sabotaged my 80 for my 20, now I'm losing out.

Love is what moved them in; my immaturity has moved them out.

To the brothers that have a rider, one that's true no doubt:

Put a ring on shorty's finger; trust me, these hoes you can do without.

She Left Me

She left me. She said I was too soft.

I tried to provide what I thought she wanted inside: a glimpse of truth, in a world full of lies.

My goal was to penetrate her mentally, as well as I did her thighs.

She left me.

She said she wanted "a real nigga."

I attempted to assimilate, grew a beard, loosened my belt, but deep down inside, I realized that I was losing myself.

She left me.

She traded the college student for a hustler with fast money and a passport.

She said getting back with me would be like a nigga in jail giving up his last "Port."

She left me.

I questioned God. What did I do to deserve this?

The low self-esteem version of me appraised my value and labeled me worthless.

She was looking for immediate gratification and materialistic forms of affection.

When I couldn't accommodate her needs, I was introduced to rejection.

In a moment of reflection, our lives were headed in different directions.

She wanted money, I wanted affection. I wish my heart came with protection.

She left me.

With no rhyme or particular reason, it was the beginning of summer; they say this time of year is usually the season.

What she did to my heart was a war crime and she needs to be brought up on charges of treason.

She traded poems in the park, for Sunday shopping at Bloomie's and Neiman's.

She regrets me. She said I was her biggest mistake.

I feel like I'm the one who fell victim to falling for a fake.

She never cared about how much I loved her, only the amount of money I stood to make.

She left me. Truthfully, it was probably a blessing.

True love should be a stress reliever,

not the main reason you are stressing.

I Ain't Him

I ain't him.

I'm not the 4 years of work. I'm graduation.

I'm the celebration after years of frustration.

I'm your savior. Not necessarily biblical.

Rather a mixture of mental and physical. I'm food for the soul. He was cereal.

I'm not into material. Though I see the materials you posses.

I'm not talking hips, lips, thighs, or breasts.

I'm talking what real men do what's right for, and why boys get left.

I'm next.

I'm the reason everyone who came before me never worked out.

My only desire is to inspire your heart to love again, by putting in time and pulling the hurt out.

I can't say for sure if we're going to work out, but don't knock it till you try it.

My destination is greatness, love, and I could use a co-pilot.

Let's be fly together. Let's try together.

Let our hearts beat as one in unison so deeply that when you take your last breath, I'm without air and we die together.

Now that I've told you what I am, let me remind you what I am not.

I'm not an ATM, personal cab, or just an addition to the pot.

I'm not the one you call when he acts stupid. I'm the reason it's him you no longer call.

I won't treat you like 'sum her' until winter. Since I've got you sprung, it's only right I be there when you fall,

for me.

Trust me, I'll catch you. Use every muscle to protect you.

I'll give you all the space in the world, but never neglect you.

The games he played made you die a thousand deaths. Let my maturity resurrect you.

Who am I?

Not perfect. Not complete. Not innocent or without sin,

I'm also not here to waste your time.

More importantly,

I ain't him.

Man-friend

Let's hold off on having sex as long as possible.

I want to love what's inside before I love your insides.

Even though your body's calling me, I refuse to pick up.

If I drink too fast from the waters you supply, I might hiccup.

Temptation has my heart racing.

This is too important for me to choke. Your love is addictive, it's got me skit'zin; I call it dope.

Let's take it slow girl. I want you to give it to me when you're ready.

The look in your eye will let me know girl.

Let's go girl.

Where lovers call ecstasy.

I promise to do it right and give you whatever is left of me.

Is it weird if I tell you I want it to be more than just sex to me?

When we're done, it wouldn't feel right if after you come back from the bathroom, you didn't get in bed and lay next to me.

Instead of the awkward moment when you're confused about what to do next.

Let's do dinner, let's do dates, let's do church, before we do sex.

You can keep your "boyfriend," I'm interested in being your man-friend.

The type to talk you through your problems, give you advice,
encourage-your-plans-friend.

The benefits of my presence are never limited to penetration.

I want you to be a goal digger.

While I make love to your aspirations.

The beauty I see in you is more than physical, so sex is irrelevant.

The man in me won't let me be called “boyfriend.”

Let’s fall in love while being celibate.

"Boyfriend" is just a title, a label or introduction.

A term simple minds use to categorize those they are lusting.

I crave a title much greater.

A boy would show you off as his new toy, I want to proclaim my
love for you to my creator.

Our love will never be secret, known from Catalina to Camden.

So either you can keep your boyfriend or give me the privilege of
being your man-friend.

Not Even Close

So you're a man because you've got a couple grand?

Because you keep a couple women in the palm of your hand?

Well, I'll be damned.

Don't confuse money with maturity, age with intellect; it's easier to give money than it is to get respect.

Just because you call yourself hard, and certain portions of your physical can become erect—these things are irrelevant in the presence of women; in order to cum often, you must come correct.

Correct isn't writing a check, so take notes and make the corrections.

Being a man is about support; so provide her protection, provide her affection, inspire aggression, light a fire in her because being a man is not firing weapons.

Too many boys think they're men, when they're really professional children.

Assuming that how you sex and how you dress are what's best and appealing.

They're not in touch with their feelings. They *must* use the drugs they are dealing.

Ruth Chris for their muses, but excuses when it's time to take out their children.

Quality over quantity, there isn't always strength in numbers.

Half breeds are men in winter and spring break is when they awake to pimp in the summer.

Whose direction are you under? You're a follower and not a leader. Your penis is not the only muscle strong enough to feed her.

Your mouth says you want her, but your actions don't reflect that you need her.

No matter how many dimes you got in your pocket, that's not the type of change that feeds the man meter.

How are you a man if you beat her? How are you a man if you cheat her?

How are you a man if restraining orders make for 3rd party supervision when you meet her?

You're not a man. Even being called "boy" would be an accomplishment.

Men are self-aware—boys need compliments and acknowledgement.

Don't confuse the fact that some women are meek with them being passive and tolerant.

It's only in the presence of boys that a real woman has fear of being dominant.

Pump Your Brakes

Slow down Sweetheart.

What's the reason you're rushing? Is it the compliments about your face that have you smiling and constantly blushing?

Is it because he's older? More mature? Not afraid to spend his money? Is that what has you crushing?

It's here today and gone tomorrow and what are you left with? NOTHING.

Slow down sweetheart; don't move too fast. Your youth is your greatest asset.

Don't feel pressure because all of your girlfriends are wild and you haven't "given up no ass" yet.

Slow down sweetheart.

Not for me, please do it for yourself.

For between your thighs lies a prize more valuable than wealth.

Now experience is cool when making love, and sometimes it might even help.

Though when conversations are had regarding the number of past partners. The closer it is to zero makes grown men melt!

Slow down sweetheart.

It's not too late. If he's the man he appears to be, he won't mind the wait.

Be mindful of the type of men you let eat from your plate.

Some would rather skip dinner and go straight for your cake.

After being fed, you'll be full, and put on a little weight.

You've now lost that figure that got you on those dates.

All that love that was meant to be has transformed to hate.

Just when you think you're going to spin, your cycle is two months late.

Now you can't slow down sweetheart. In fact, you've got to move even faster.

Four years from now you'll have a Bachelor's degree in being a mom,

when you should be working on your Masters.

Slow down sweetheart.

For like fast money, fast girls get treated the same.

So I feel it's only right that I fly you this kite,

so at least you now know the game.

Poetic Justice

To the deaths that go unpublicized and the marches for which no feet paced.

Allow me to offer some poetic justice that my words may be used in their place.

One life lost is more than one life altered; some deaths change entire communities.

How can one murder leave you outraged and appalled, and to others you have some sort of immunity?

Society is filled with casual people, in casual dress, who have casual sex.

While causal may suffice for their casual lifestyle, one should never be casual of death.

As I watch these buffet activists choose which sides to embrace with acknowledgement,

I think of the other lives lost this year and question their motives with astonishment.

March today. March tomorrow. March till your feet become callused.

March even when you must march alone; it only takes two feet to break silence.

Some will digest this food I'm delivering, others will resort to purging.

I'm not here to judge anyone's previous transgressions. I'm just planning for the days that are emerging.

Another murder will happen quite soon; this time, much closer to home.

If its protest isn't labeled the cool thing to do,

will its details still be displayed on your phone?

The answer of course is probably not, no Tweegrams, or posts, or letters to cops.

No hoodies or t-shirts or walking down blocks.

Just the shutting of windows and turning of locks.

If this is the case, then don't march at all.

Resort to business as usual and visit the mall.

Party with friends, live it up, have a ball.

Just pray when the next murder happens it won't be your number that's called.

However, if march you must, please wear your hoodie.

Make sure you pull tightly on the strings.

If you don't march forward for each murder after,

your being there doesn't mean a thing.

Mr. Rebound

I hate being Mr. Rebound when your last boyfriend broke your heart.

You really don't feel like dating, yet all your girlfriends say it's time to start.

I know it's him you think of, instead of me, when we're apart.

It doesn't feel right, like food shopping with a broken cart.

He fucked up, then I lucked up, but am I really lucky? She tells me stories of how he beat her and the visions disgust me.

She warned me, "I'll go to jail before I let another nigga touch me."

Now she drowns her sorrow in Peach Ciroc, courtesy of Puffy.

It's not my fault he didn't tell you that you were beautiful, or that he was only pursuing you to quench his thirst for doing you.

After doing you, his colors became true to you, and now you're dead on the inside, while your soul is the undertaker for your heart's funeral.

Now it's up to me to prove to her that some men are different. That's a lot of pressure.

Since my own heart is on life support and my soul is on a stretcher.

More importantly though, I'm a man so it's in my nature to provide and protect her, listen when she's talking, put in time, and never neglect her.

I hate being Mr. Rebound when the last man wasn't man enough.

It's not my fault he left you with a son to teach about "manning up."

That's ignorantly ironic, but much more, it's actuality.

He sold her a dream that never manifested itself into reality.

I hate being Mr. Rebound, but I'm going to take the role and play it well.

It's working because he texted her: "IMU" and her response was: "go to hell."

"I've got a new man now and he treats me rather well. Oh, and you better pay your child support pretty soon or you're going to jail."

I still hate being Mr. Rebound, but it's good to see my woman's progression.

Now the bedroom is the only place I see her aggression.

To her ex, I'm Mr. Rebound. To her son, I'm just Mr. Mike.

To me, she is the world, and to her I am

Mr. Right.

Dear Ex-Girlfriend

I hope this letter finds you in good spirits because the demons are with me.

I finally ran into that woman you said you sent for me.

(K) Because it's killing me that I sacrificed love for women who just wanted to be able to hold something above you.

(A) Because I was too arrogant to see the error in my ways; we could lay up under each other for days, but as soon as you left my presence, I found it pleasurable to disrespect you. Not thinking how my actions would affect you.

(R) Because I knew right from wrong; you would make love to me so long that Pandora ran out of songs—but the second you wanted to take a night off, to just hold each other with the lights off, my immaturity led me to whichever girl was willing to take her tights off.

(M) Because I was supposed to be your man. You put your heart in my hand and instead of playing my cards right, I chose to fold. I pictured us together, growing old. Now the left side of my bed is 'winter-in-Chicago' cold. We're supposed to be in this together, my immaturity is the reason we're not. You've moved on with your life and I'm still here, stuck in the same spot.

I failed you. When I should've gotten an (A).

The karma of screwing over a good girl is watching her walk away.

Not being able to do anything about it.

Once having had every opportunity to make her stay.

You're supposed to build a home where there is a foundation,
not wherever you decide to lay.

I went from being a rolling stone, to rolling in the deep.

While you we counting sheep, I was counting the woman with
whom I planned to creep.

I just want you to know that karma has caught up with me.

I sold you out and she is my price to pay.

If I'd believed in her when you told me she was real, then you'd
probably be my wife today.

Love and Basketball

I don't know why you're playing hard to get.

We haven't even started yet. Your name isn't Madison, but you can't recall the last time one of these Squares got your Garden wet.

I'm not cocky, but how I put the full court press on, not even a backcourt of Kobe and Iverson in '05 could stop me.

You never really did Phil him, but the Jackson's made up for his lack of attraction.

No matter how many pairs of heels you own, a good pair of ball sneaks will give you your best opportunity to maintain traction.

Mark my words: even if you were with him shooting in the Jim, that doesn't make the relationship even Stephen.

He could still break your heart and take his talent elsewhere, like when number 23 left Cleveland.

You made a rookie mistake. You jumped right into it out of high school, made yourself available in the upcoming draft.

You thought the streets taught you all you needed to know about love, when in reality you could've used a college class.

To the brothers that get recruited harder than Jesus Shuttlesworth:

They'll eat you for breakfast using sex as the weapon—steer clear of Mrs. Buttersworth.

Everything that looks good isn't good for you.

When you shine like Lebron, it's hard to differentiate the foil from the loyal.

Like basketball, you cannot achieve greatness in love without practice.

The two of you need to be on the same page of the playbook, before you take it to the mattress.

Safety first. You don't have to go to USC to play with Trojans.

If you don't, you'll be sicker than Magic Johnson, or over before you start, like Greg Oden.

Before you make her a Basketball Wife, see how she acts as a fiancé.

That's the difference between keeping Amil, or sitting court side like Beyoncé.

Sometimes it's all about the ring, like Ray Allen in Miami.

Sometimes the ring may not mean a thing, like Kim Zoliack or Tammy.

The Best for Last

Keep hope alive.

They're all going to be your ex when God sends you your husband.

The best way to know when you are truly happy is to be able to reflect on when you wasn't.

Don't be sad that it happened. Be grateful it's over.

I know at night it gets colder, and your heart's growing older—

Just be patient, sometimes life has to introduce you to the enemy first, so you can recognize when you've found a soldier.

Find a man who isn't intimated by your independence and intelligence.

One who can manipulate your mind and body in ways that would have you testifying that before him, you must have been celibate.

They're out here, just a little less apparent—not as easily noticed.

He'll send you flowers because you're the bomb, and he'll call you his Lotus.

Don't sell yourself short by selling yourself.

"He's going to change one day." That's what you keep telling yourself.

Go and better yourself. Why are you waiting for change?

You can't fall in love with players and expect them to not be feeding you game.

While he's feeding you game, your appetite, it wants more.

If people show you their ass, it's best you show them the door.

Furthermore, let the doorknob hit them on the way out.

Don't get played waiting for the situation to play out.

Only then would the man of your dreams request his entry.

He won't be afraid of your scars; his hands will heal them gently.

You keep hope alive because at the end of the day, there isn't too much more you are left with.

Life's puzzle comes with many pieces; it's up to you to find the best fit.

Love Making

Damn, have we all forgotten how to make love?

I don't mean satisfying wetness and erections with giving it up and putting it in whoever is ready with protection.

I'm talking about affection.

Where bodies meet between sheets and souls collide.

Where bathroom breaks feel like eternity and you grow cold inside.

I'm not talking about "gettin' it in real quick" before you part ways and begin the rest of your evening.

I'm talking about paralyzing love making, so comforting that even a natural disaster wouldn't prevent you from leaving.

We've perverted love making, renaming it a "fuck."

Now we're doing it for curiosity, attention and a buck.

Now we do it to acquire love, not to show our lover appreciation.

If you're not in love, you can't make love.

So just call it penetration.

Young girls haven't even stepped into womanhood yet, but have stepped out of virginity.

If you can handle criticism, then I'm here to tell you what you're doing is stupidity.

Are you kidding me?

Young men inquire about what's between thighs before searching for what's behind eyes.

Older women convince themselves that their partners have earned the title of lover to rationalize rewarding them with love's prize.

Behind door number one: a bedroom full of lies.

Flirt with love through text messages and provocative pictures.

Provoke love prematurely due to fears of being replaced by "freak bitches."

When these are really the "weak bitches," female dogs surely.

Love-making is the transcendence of a relationship.

Not verification of maturity.

Love-making has lost its purity.

Some cowards have stooped so low as to try to take it.

Remember,

the key to amazing love is falling in it before you make it.

Miss Misguided

Too many women want to be bad, not enough want to be beautiful.

Too many tolerate bullshit and disrespect as the usual.

You can't expect respect, with no respect for yourself.

Too many chase checks and check for a nigga, without checking for self.

Not to mention she lives at the mall, but she also lives with mommy.

She spends her last on fashion, desperately in need of a hobby.

Tory Burch has a home. Gucci has two. If you keep investing in them, who's investing in you?

The majority of their lives, they've tried being something they weren't.

Everyone who tried to school them on the error of their ways, were told they were "fuckin buggin'."

Life is sometimes plagued with the curse of false intelligence.

Not enough women want to be happy. Too many women want to be relevant.

Popularity is pressure. Pressure bursts pipes.

Don't let pressure make you a mother.

Before love makes you wife.

Pressure makes young minded women want to learn how to give head right.

Instead of trying to get their head right.

To find "a nigga with his bread right."

You think that having good head is going to get you bread?

Clearly, you weren't bred right!

Young girl lost. I pray the right guy finds you.

Before the compliments about your ass get you big headed and blind you.

This is a reminder, selling yourself will never be as valuable as self-worth.

So before you try loving a nigga, try loving yourself first.

Play your cards right, take the hand you were dealt first.

Before you start giving your love, make sure your feelings are felt first.

The Good Guy Blues

The hardest part about being a good man is finding a good woman.

That doesn't mean she's good in the bedroom, good at cleaning or good looking.

What happened to the good girls? The ones who aren't in a rush to grow up?

The ones who don't chase men with shots of liquor, till they throw up?

The ones who don't get goosebumps when the fellas talk and bring "some hoe" up.

One, who when we talk about body count, she be all hype and throw a 4 up.

I'm looking for a good girl. Good job, good hair, and good credit.

One who doesn't need a reality check, or a joint account from which to debit.

I was never stingy with money; a penny not saved will be eventually wasted.

Time is a different type of money, one you can't bargain or trade with.

I get up and go to work every day because I believe it's a man's job to support his woman.

She calls me "the last of the gentlemen." I'm about respecting, protecting and courting women.

You can waste my food; all four burners are lit on most evenings.

I'll even pack your lunch while you're in the shower because I know you're always in a rush when you're leaving.

Just don't waste my time, there's no market on Earth that sells it.

Any question that needs an answer, be observant because time tells it.

Time has shown me, the older you get, fewer options are present.

The women who were curious of loves "once upon a time," now live with resentment.

Some with emotional scars, some with real ones, and most with dependents and fathers who don't fulfill their obligations to their mate or descendants.

I don't want the most beautiful, the richest, or even the flyest—

Just one who won't give up on love before trying it.

As much as I want to deny it, it's clearer to me the further I proceed.

Finding a good woman is almost impossible and that's one more impossibility I don't need.

Frenemies

Fake friends are worse than real enemies.

Be careful who you let in, people will use you for your energy.

Make sure you do your homework. Don't ever take them home first.

Nosey neighbors are worse than investigators; they're taking notes of how your home works.

Don't share your past with them, it's class to them.

Bring them around your man, they'll kindly smile in his face but behind closed doors, give their ass to him.

They'll borrow your shoes.

Then, they'll borrow a purse.

Then, they'll borrow your boyfriend,

That's how borrowing works.

Men aren't too much different. Everything's a competition.

Watch out for boys that try to shit and piss on your dreams,

but don't have a pot to piss in.

Or a window to throw it out.

Fake friends you can go without.

There's a significant difference between a rider,

and somebody that's always around when you're rolling out.

It's not a about who was there first, it's about who's there every time you need them.

There's a difference between eating off your plate and eating with you, don't ever feed them.

The greedy bite hands when getting fed and snakes are visible when the grass is cut.

If their presence doesn't add value, then their absence shouldn't make you give a fuck.

The Love Game

If you feel like playing games go to Dave and Busters.

It's hard when a good man comes around, and she doesn't trust you.

I don't blame her as much as I blame the boys that came before me. I'm tired of meeting women who share the same damn story.

Meet a guy, like a guy, give him some, then watch him change up.

When you met him he was in the street, but you think you can make him give the game up.

You think you're flying with an eagle, but time reveals he's a lame duck.

You wish he had showed you this side of him before you gave it up and gave a fuck.

Men belong with women, so let niggas have the hoes, and when these opposites cross paths, someone's going to run quicker than cheap panty-hoes.

Women want respect, while it's 'bout checks for your average hoe. Men look you in the eye, while a nigga's gaze is toward your camel toe.

To each his own.

We need hoes to keep niggas occupied. So niggas don't rob men of women, like Africa and Amistad.

I used to be a nigga myself, so my words have a history, but how men can fall in love with hoes will forever be a mystery.

Women hold you down, hoes hold you up. Women give their all, hoes give a nut.

Niggas give one too, men give their last. Women give advice, hoes just give their ass.

It's what you do between screws that nails down your position. Are you really making love? Or are these acts of contrition?

Sex isn't better than love; they're not even in the same ballpark. That's like comparing Piaget and Erickson, or Target and Walmart.

The problem is thinking that as men and women, we must pick and choose.

Why can't we just catch them all and ride with one like Pikachu?

This isn't a game; hoes would think I'm talking Pokémon.

Men will pick and poke your brain, while niggas would try and poke your mom.

On its face, this poem may be trivial, but the situation is rather serious.

To keep it short and sweet, save our women. Period.

Preparation

What good is Mr. Right, if Ms. Right isn't ready to meet him?

Don't confuse the streets' interpretation of love; you're going to need more than vagina to feed him.

Want him, don't need him.

Make him spoil you, but don't bleed him.

Make time to remove the cobwebs from your closet before you open your door to greet him.

She's great in bed, but can't make rice to save her life.

Since her ass is fat, I'm supposed to save her, right?

She knows how to ride it.

That does me no good; I need somebody I can ride with.

A 'stand up' woman, more than someone I can lie with.

The head is good, and she knows how to roll the weed up.

If that makes you wifey material, I guarantee you'll sign a prenup.

Let your greatest features be your intellect and assets.

Real men won't even notice you haven't given up any "ass" yet.

Don't be chased, but be pursued. Be vocal, but not rude.

Let him successfully undress your mind, before he sees you in the nude.

Take the time to better yourself. Mice look for cheese. Have cheddar yourself.

When you begin to look for Mr. Right, don't begin with makes or models or letters on belts.

Keep your clothes on when you advertise yourself; pictured publicity stunts could hurt you.

The finest of rides are never advertised, remind me of a time you've seen a Bentley commercial.

Appreciate the single you, but prepare for love while you do it.

The last thing you want to happen is love's candle to burn gently in your face and you blew it.

Fall in love with self.

Then fall in love with single.

You can't fall in love with monogamy,

until you fall out of love with mingle.

Let's Wait

Am I wrong if I tell you that I want to make love to your mind first?

Before giving back shots that sweat out hair and make spines hurt.

I want to make you mine first.

I want to put in time first.

I want to eat outside before I devour your insides, I don't want dessert. I want to dine first.

Can we have a glass of wine first? Act like kids and bump and grind first?

Don't spoil the pleasure of anticipation, leave the lights on,

I want to see you shine first.

I'm already impressed with your body; I want you to show me how your mind works.

What makes you focused, how your grind works, before I make your inner thighs hurt.

Postpone the climax for the end of our love movie; don't give it to me in the intro.

For now, your beautiful face is the only place I'm checking for a dimple.

Having sex is simple; making love is for grown men. Let's build a relationship with God first, if eventually we're going to sin.

This is a message from a grown man, who knows what love feels like.

Let's not do it when our bodies tell us,

but when our hearts and minds say it feels right.

I'm just praying it feels tight because loose lips sink ships.

Weak walls makes houses tumble and fall.

So don't pick up the phone when your body calls.

Don't be afraid of your body's flaws; imperfection is the purest perfect.

Perfect is not what I ask you to be, only loyal, honest and worth it.

So baby, can we wait a while? I promise you it's better.

For when waters run with no place to go, the end result is something wetter.

Royalty

The problem with most queens is they mistake the jokers for the kings. Searching for wealth instead of health, they focus on material things.

Understand that you are a queen and should be treated as if you were royalty. I mean, the fact that he buys you shit is cool, but there is no price tag on loyalty.

Love could never be blind enough because we are fixated on the superficial.

Disappointments hit you like missiles; your Louie bag should have come with tissues.

This is the life you have subscribed to. Everyone wants to be like the girl in the magazine, but nobody wants the issues.

You know that you have found your king when he respects you like his mother.

Protects you like his sister, before inquiring about becoming your lover.

To some this might sound lame, but that depends on the type of brother.

If you agree with me and he doesn't, then it's a fine time for you to find another.

Next time you go looking, remember you are what you attract, everyone these days will come with baggage, find someone willing to help you unpack.

Women 101

See, women are a math problem that I have a problem "mathin'."

Since back when dictionaries and calculators were code words when kids were "mackin'."

How are we going take from each other and expect addition?

Our problems will continue to multiply, if there is always division.

We let outsiders influence our equation. We call them exponents. We should be 1+1 when facing our opponents.

We're just different. My soul is in turmoil, like Billie Holiday in strange fruit.

I say I'm trying to live right and you're calling it the square route.

I'm just trying to be good and good for you, like Chinese food and Clear Fruit.

I guess I should have given you compliments, like "nice dress" and "your hair is cute."

I shouldn't have jumped out of this airplane without an instructor and a parachute.

I shouldn't have let those other women in because we couldn't share a coupe.

A relationship is meant for two, and people don't know how to add.

They just like subtraction better because watching people go through stuff makes them glad.

Word of advice: if you've got a wife, don't let the world in.

You might think she just wants to blow you, but homewreckers come with whirlwinds.

If you think algebra's hard, try a month without your woman giving you any action.

I guarantee you, like the big joker, you'll wish she'd forget that addition and start subtraction.

You've got the classic wintertime love, but when the weather changed you became a summer fool.

You didn't appreciate what you had all winter, now she's got you in summer school.

All of this because you didn't pay attention to Tyler Perry and his 80/20 ratio.

Now her class you didn't pass because you ditched the final for a little fellatio.

The Thrill of the Chase

Don't be so caught up on chasing women that you forget to keep the one who already chose you.

A loyal woman deserves way more respect than any of the hoes do.

Why get a second job when you can put in overtime at the first one?

She knows you're going to make mistakes, but cheating on her is the worst one.

Not everybody cheats, if they did, it wouldn't be called cheating.

Watching your Queen walk out of your life is more painful than any Rodney King beating.

It's not her fault she's pretty, it's your fault that pretty is all you see.

Instead of wanting her to be arm candy, give her what she needs, so she can be all she can be.

Her "pretty" makes you insecure. That's not love, that's pretty immature.

You can call it whatever you want to, but pretty soon, she'll call a man for your child's play cure.

It's hard enough to be pretty in a world full of haters.

Don't make it hard to be pretty at home.

Pretty soon she'll find someone who looks past the pretty, and you will be pretty alone.

I bet chasing isn't as much fun because instead of chasing you're replacing;

You run around like you're a love doctor when you should be practicing patience.

Besides being pretty beautiful, she's actually pretty intelligent.

When you screw over those who keep you nailed down, the end result pretty celibate.

Everything that looks good isn't good for you, and anything that comes easy, isn't worth keeping.

Don't let what you do with a hoe be the reason your housewife is leaving.

The Other Side of Bed

No one likes sleeping alone, but don't let that make you invite a
stranger into your home.

The other side of your bed is a privilege, only kings and queens
should be rewarded a throne.

Don't let your desire for body heat make you bring just anybody
between your sheets because

between me and you, somebody might confuse your loneliness
with being somebody's freak.

My advice is to get a bigger blanket, some thicker socks and
some pajamas.

They shouldn't be allowed to stay till the sun comes up if they're
not worthy of meeting your mama.

They invented body pillows if you need something to roll over
and hold onto.

Only little children are scared to sleep alone—"manning up" is
what the grown do.

If you're scared of the dark, sleep with the lights on; if it gets too
chilly throw sweatpants or tights on.

If they try something that you're not comfortable with, you
might be in for a run for your money, so put some Mike's on.

Bed bugs aren't the only thing that you should worry about
when sleeping in strange places.

I know you might miss your significant other, but sleep alone until you find a significant replacement.

Being drunk is not an excuse; if the Patron made you do it, then sleep with the bottle.

HIV doesn't have occupational exemptions, it's found in both ball players and models.

Whomever you choose to sleep with should be worthy enough for you to wake up to.

While you might just want to be held, they might have every intention of trying to screw you.

Leeches

Sometimes you have to leave people where they are for you to get where you are going.

If you keep taking food out of your own mouth to feed the hunger of others, then don't be surprised when you're not growing.

Some peoples' purpose is for a season and we keep them around for centuries. We must not waste what we don't have in abundance like time, tears, and energy.

When givers meet takers what's really taken is advantage.

There is motivation in eating steak dinners in front of those whose situation only affords a sandwich.

Poverty by complacency is laziness, and shouldn't be awarded with nourishment.

There are other ways to feed people, try tough love or encouragement.

Doctors cut umbilical cords; breastfeeding is replaced by bottles. Yes, Jesus fed the poor, but he also made fisherman of the Apostles.

Just because they have the weight of models, doesn't mean you should put them up on your shoulders.

Sleeping with the enemy makes you a prisoner of war; you are definitely destiny's child, but not necessarily a solider.

Field Nigger

Where are all the role models? The ones who celebrate success without the need for a gold bottle.

Someone so cold that even the old could follow.

Society is devouring our youth; these streets eat you alive and you'll get whole-swallowed.

We desire to be what we see, but it seems to me our vision is clouded.

The number of people that notice the need for change is far greater than those actively doing something about it.

We must provide our youth with other options.

There's a difference between toasting to our social successes, and random bottle popping.

We must level the playing field. Monogamy and matrimony have become extinct; everybody wants to play the field.

We must educate that education can also be your emancipation,

not just how well you shoot a ball, or play the field.

For centuries, owners have reaped the rewards of how well we've used our athleticism to slave in fields.

Martin Luther was a King, as was Rodney, but now the joke's on us, these street are a danger-field.

The playing fields have just been shifted from the plantation to the arena.

It's a jungle out here, where are the Mufasas to protect our Simbas from the hyenas?

Harriet Tubman could have freed many more slaves if they'd only known they were captives.

Free rides to college because of physical skill have not produced enough Bachelors.

Not nearly enough minorities with their Masters, but we are still slaves to our masters' control.

We just spend more on our chains now because they have blood diamonds and they're gold.

Our leaders are getting old. It's time for us to properly train our replacements.

Our biggest inspirations have become rappers,

while executives reside in high rises and the Tiggers and niggers are in the basement.

Gone, But Not Forgotten

Not many know what you are going through.

I don't believe the word that describes how you feel at this moment has been invented yet.

When a precious life is snatched far too soon, it is impossible to be accepting of death,

when the life taken had not begun living yet.

Please allow me to offer my condolences, and ask that while you shed tears from the loss,

let your tissues be the happy moments.

Let your memories be the energy to give you strength at the weakest of times.

Storm clouds are never forever, eventually the sun will shine.

May its rays shine brighter for you, now that you have experienced a different type of darkness.

For it will take a brave heart to understand that we must not let our joy be taken by the heartless.

Healing is a process with no timetable or remedy.

Although the life taken cannot be replaced, we can reflect upon the memories.

May its reflection provide you protection, as life from today onward is forever different.

Understand that while you may not have been ready, there is a higher power that has a mission.

Trust that the plan is not mistaken; peace will come, please be patient.

Even the most precious of flowers will not last forever, but may you always remember their fragrance.

How to Date

Since when does getting a phone number mean you're getting some?

Since when does what you get become more important than who you get it from?

Sex is not a right, it's not required, it's a reward.

How can you expect to be given an allowance without completing all the chores?

Dating requires patience. Dating requires time. Dating requires communication and stimulation of the mind.

If she doesn't make you work for it, when she gives it to you it won't be appreciated.

The race is over before it's begun; you're left feeling dumb like, "Damn, I wish I'd waited."

I bet you wish you'd dated, or made a promise to yourself to be more than penetrated.

It's love that you're looking for, I bet you wish you'd made it.

Make love, not mistakes. Be friends first, and then date.

Too often people skip dinner, pick up the dessert menu and request cake.

They don't understand the pleasures associated with patience and perseverance.

Or the passion of infatuation; we are deeper than personal appearance.

You date by phone conversations, asking questions and learning behaviors.

Dating is not inviting them over prematurely because you want their name known by your neighbors.

A man only achieves what you allow them to. Don't bend or readjust the bar. Instead find a mate that meets it.

Better yet one that exceeds your expectations without you first giving them a reason.

Know When to Go

It's time.

You will never achieve victory, if you allow yourself to remain the victim.

You know it could have been worse right?

You could have wasted another year with him.

You could have had another baby, another set of bruises from another fight.

You could have spent another Sunday evaluating why love didn't make him come home another Saturday night.

What defines you is what happens after you've been broken.

Let what could have had the power to break you ultimately make you, the chooser is far more powerful than the chosen.

Sometimes not coming at all is better than coming second.

When being content with less than what you deserve is used against you as a weapon.

If you tolerate bullshit, don't be upset when it reappears.

Never cry for someone who won't stick around to wipe away the tears.

Don't let your fear of being lonely make you settle for a piece of someone.

Pieces are what your heart will be in when your piece says peace to be with their #1.

#2's sing the blues. How do you expect to get what you deserve if you are just taking what you can get?

If I were you I would leave now, take nothing but your pride and respect.

No need to look back, your entire future is in front of you.

You should never do what you are told if it's not exactly what you want to do.

When the actions that were displayed when they wanted you have disappeared once you surrendered,

you can no longer be their present, rather someone that they remember.

So choose to love again, but this time, learn from what "bad love" has taught you.

There's another love story that must be written about where what once broke you down has brought you.

It's a Man's World

If you're not making her better, then by default, she's worse off being with you.

The requirement for keeping a woman is not great sex, and texts saying, "I miss you."

You don't have to be rich, but every woman needs a man with his life together.

It is essential for you to have a plan and a purpose if you're going to prove to her you're worth being with forever.

You do not necessarily have to "trick," but from time to time every woman deserves to be treated.

Support, trust, stability, and respect, are just some of the qualities that are needed.

You must prove to her that you're a leader, if you request that it's you she must follow.

It's said that a woman's husband replaces her father as a provider, protector, and role model.

You must lead by example, bend occasionally, but never so much that you'd break.

You must be a man of your word. Let your actions speak louder and keep every promise you make.

Keep the outsiders at bay, for your woman is prey, by both males and females who envy.

What good is establishing a home, if you seek shelter elsewhere—as quick as it was filled with love, it can be emptied.

Never underestimate the independence of a woman.

Realize that she can be successful alone.

Understand that your success is not hers to covet; a real woman wants to be successful on her own.

Don't let your insecurity lead to possessiveness and insecurity. Confidence wears as well as clean shaves and tailored suits.

It's a man's world surely, but women are what make it go 'round.

It's your obligation to constantly build her up and be there for her if ever it goes down.

The difference between "for now" and forever is getting too comfortable and complacency.

Never present a woman with problem that must be handled any way, other than gracefully.

Child Support

"I mean, at least I pay Child Support."

Pardon me if I laugh.

Enlighten me on how you can effectively support a child with maybe one night a week and some cash?

A father's place is in the home, not his own, but with the mother.

Every opportunity and ounce of effort must be exhausted before you proceed with another.

You went half on the baby, so go half on the responsibility.

How are you now somehow selfish with your time and money, when she wasn't selfish with her fertility?

Half is just the minimum; a real man takes on the majority.

Tell me more about how your new girlfriend and her two kids are now the priority.

If you didn't really love her, then you shouldn't have planted your seed in her garden.

Now it has grown to be precious Earth while you're presence is unidentifiable, Marvin the Martin.

Finish what you started, be dearly beloved, not dearly departed.

It's not her new boyfriend's responsibility to pick up where you left off; it's your child too, so please support it.

Don't let court mandates dictate the frequency of visitation.

Especially when you showed up faster than delivery men when the agenda was penetration.

Now all of a sudden it's "not your weekend," and "I gotta see if my mom can take him."

Your mama did not make him. When you fall through the cracks, it eventually breaks him.

A man you must make him.

That can't be done with a sleepover every other Saturday, staying up late, and letting him chew gum.

You must be consistent with the discipline, don't disregard mom's authority to be the cool one.

Don't be excited about Father's Day if you haven't done anything the other 364 days.

What your son needs is his father around more, not more video games and more Jays.

Please don't think that a child support check and a goodnight phone call makes you a hero.

If you add it all up the amount of support you're really giving your child is almost zero.

Man Up

My Brother, you have a job to do.

Don't let your nightmares get in the way of your dreams.

Don't let your thirst for cream, force you to resort to schemes.

Convince the world you're not color blind. Stop killing and spilling innocent red in an effort to acquire green.

That isn't what Mr. X meant when he said "by any means." Dreams are the foundation for your future.

You're the future.
Men who came before you died to protect.
RIP Martin Luther.

So all the bullshit you must overcome. We must return the favor and love women. Not kill each other over something dumb.

It's hard to learn being a man, when you have no real men around you.

You talk about doing something other than "getting money and fucking bitches" and those around you only clown you.

The pressure of being popular and impressing women has you stressing.

When you don't have a teacher to guide you, you're left with just the streets to give you lessons.

You must realize that the street is a last resort. Not a priority.

There isn't always strength in numbers. When the conversation is incarceration, young Black men are the majority.

You're looking for a way out; all you see is bricks and basketballs,

but sports were never your thing, and riding dirty will have you
6 feet under dirt.

You must understand that your last brick won't move because
it's on top of where your casket falls.

Credits

First, I would like to thank God for blessing me with the desire to write. My only hope is that the gift he has blessed me with will bless the lives of others.

Second, I would like to thank all of my family and friends for the support and encouragement that lead me to write what I feel, in an effort to change the way you do.

A special thanks to My Mother, (Charlene Reid) My Editor (Meloni C. Williams) Joel, Dan, Shante, Tiasha, Cyber Tourniquet, and everyone who pushed me to bring you:

"Just Words."

This is my first book, but I promise, it will not be my last.